WALK ON

FROM THE VALLEY OF DESPAIR
TO THE MOUNTAINTOP OF PRAISE

RON BRACY

Published by Carpenter's Son Publishing, Franklin, Tennessee
Editor Gail Fallen, cover and interior Design by Debbie Manning Sheppard

All Scripture quotations, unless otherwise indicated, are from the
New American Standard Bible, The Lockman Founation,
A.J. Holman Company: Philadelphia and New York, 1960.
Scripture quotations marked NASB are from the New American Standard Bible.
Scripture quotations marked ESV are from the English Standard Version.
Scripture quotations marked KJV are from the King James Version.
Scripture quotations marked NIV are from the New International Version.
Scripture quotations marked NKHV are from the New King James Version.

Special recognition to Mr. Geoff Pleasance of the United Kingdom
who granted permission to use the drawing "Sharing the Sky" of the
MC-130H Combat Talon airplane on the memorial page of *Walk On*.
Mr. Pleasance, a noted military aviation artist,
is an ardent friend and supporter of the United States Air Force.

WALK ON

FROM THE VALLEY OF DESPAIR TO THE MOUNTAINTOP OF PRAISE

RON BRACY

IN MEMORY

Captain Todd R. Bracy
&
the Crew of Wrath 11

What People Are Saying About This Book

"Ron Bracy has made a significant contribution to Habakkuk studies. He examines the biblical text closely to understand it in the context of the prophet's day. At the same time, his commentary is a dialogue with the ancient text which brings clarity to Habakkuk for our time. His meaningful applications of the text to contemporary lives—including his own very personal story—give readers examples as well as guidance which will allow them to discover their own personal relevance from the prophet's struggles. Bracy's work is highly recommended for those who wish to know what Habakkuk means for them today."

BOO HEFLIN
PhD, Professor Emeritus of Old Testament

*"From biblical times forward, people have questioned why God allows evil to affect our lives. By sharing the most devastating time in his life and the teachings from the Old Testament book of Habakkuk, Ron Bracy has illustrated that God is loving and all-powerful, and is still in control no matter what happens in our lives. Giving hope and encouragement, **Walk On** will truly inspire you to reach into God's Word to take you from the 'valleys' to the 'mountaintops.'"*

SARA M. SINGLETON
Retired Teacher

*"Ron Bracy's book **Walk On** offers truly inspirational reading while providing practical advice for living through the ups and downs of life. In the book, Ron tells his own gripping story of the loss of his son and his subsequent grief. Using the Old Testament book of Habakkuk as his guide, He takes us through the prophet's own despair, examines his (our) questions of God, and how God, in His time, finally answered Habakkuk. The journey's lessons are illustrated with many biblical references, Bracy's personal stories, examples from real-life people, as well as references from classical literature.*

"As a former Air Force combat fighter pilot, test pilot, and Space Shuttle astronaut, I have experienced—as most of us have—both the emotional highs of the mountain top and the dark, despairing lows in life's valleys. I, too, identified with Habakkuk's frustration, have asked God many of the same questions myself, and was comforted and inspired by the reflections in Bracy's book.

*"**Walk On** is full of practical biblical advice on how to endure and climb 'out of the valley' of life's challenges, through living by faith in God's sovereignty, having patience that God will speak and act, and persevering in our walk with the Lord."*

JOHN H. CASPER
Colonel, USAF (Ret.), NASA Astronaut; Space
Shuttle Commander, Missions STS-36, 54, 62, and 77

"Since my retirement in 2012, I have been increasingly distressed over the spiritual condition of America. Often I have asked, 'Where is God at this time of advancing evil and plateaued and declining churches?' Ron Bracy's book **Walk On** *has answered that question and enabled me to begin the journey from the Valley of Despair to the Mountaintop of Praise."*

WILLIAM S. PHILLIPS, PHD
President Emeritus, Yellowstone Christian College

"Husband, father, grandfather, minister, military veteran, teacher, and writer, Ron Bracy, in his first publication **Walk On***, gives the reader a non-fictional moving narrative of his incredible spiritual journey. Bracy charts his life's path with joys, accomplishment, confusions, despairs, anger, knowledge, and acceptance. He successfully uses humor, wisdom, brilliance of wording, and Scripture to cement his moving story.*

"Learning to trust God is difficult. The author explores and explains the Old Testament book of Habakkuk and gives examples and suggestions to illustrate both his own and the prophet's passage of life learning to accept God's infinite wisdom and truth. Bracy shows how God communicates directly with mankind often. Since God already understands our every need and desire, He has the answers—which may be dramatic or sweet, soft whispers—to guide us through life. Bracy's book makes a wonderful, powerful account of embracing one's spiritual journey."

"In his heart a man plans his course, but the Lord determines his steps."

(PROVERBS 16:9)

MARTHA MARSHALL BENTLEY
Coordinator and Instructor, Gifted, Talented, and
Creative Writing Program, Newark's School District;
Co-Owner of Marshall Dry Goods Co., Inc.

"The author, Ron Bracy, has woven together an unusual study of the Old Testament book of Habakkuk with his own personal experiences. Seldom have I read a book which touched my own emotions so profoundly. As with Habakkuk, Bracy was able to walk on because he knew that God was with him even when God seemed silent. I recommend **Walk On** *to anyone who may be undergoing difficult experience, but seemingly finds no answers from God."*

F. B. HUEY, PhD
Professor Emeritus, Southwestern Baptist
Theological Seminary

"The Old Testament book Habakkuk confronts God with questions about evil and suffering which never cease, whatever the generation. The prophet Habakkuk receives unbelievable answers which shake up his preconceived ideas. However, the prophet's honest conversations with God eventually produce in him a strengthened faith and joy in the Lord whatever the circumstances of life.

"In his book **Walk On***, author Ron Bracy describes some of the darkest events in his own life which would challenge anyone's faith. Through his study of the book of Habakkuk, Bracy reveals how the truths the prophet discovered have become incarnate in his own life.*

"Numerous illustrations of the author's encounters with hurting people in his roles as pastor, military chaplain, and teacher accentuate the result of how personal, honest conversing with God blesses life, whatever the circumstances."

JIMMIE L. NELSON, PhD
Old Testament Professor,
B.H. Carrol Theological Institute

"So you have this book in your hand. To buy or not to buy, that is the question. If you have never experienced grief, troubles, loss of any kind, anger at God, questions of God, (and who has not!), do not buy this book.

"On the other hand, when you buy **Walk On**, *you will find how the author, Ron Bracy, uses lessons from Habakkuk, the 'Prophet of the People,' to lead us to a choice of roads on which to travel the journey of life and faith. Using life experiences and God's Word, work, and presence in his own life, Bracy shows us how to walk on from the Valley of Despair to the Mountaintop of Praise.*

*"***Walk On*** is an excellent, inspiring study of the age-old questions of evil and pain, despair and sorrow. You will need a pen and a highlighter to do this book justice as you read it. May God reveal new truths and comfort to you as He did to me."*

JUDY WERNSMAN
Retired Executive Secretary; Teacher, Women's Ministry,
Hope Community Church, Brownsburg, Indiana

*"***Walk on***. These two words have more power than anyone can imagine. If anyone understands these two words, it is Ron Bracy. I strongly endorse this book. It is a great read. It is inspiring. It shows how difficult life can be. It holds no punches. Yet it also shows how to rise above any circumstance. Too many people quit too easily today. This book will show you how to walk on and fight the good fight. It will show you how to walk on and finish the race. It will show you how to walk on and keep the faith. Enjoy the read."*

JOHN VALENZUELA
Senior Pastor, MyChurch; Head Boys Basketball
Coach, San Antonio Christian

"This book and study of Habakkuk that Ron Bracy has written is one which a person should read early in their Christian walk. It will prepare them not to be shocked when tragedy and heartbreak

befall them as they walk through life. It is also a study which should be read again each time tragedy or heartbreak strikes in the life of a mature Christian. **Walk On** will serve as a reminder that God is God, and we are not. It reminds us that God still loves us and has a long-term plan for us, even if we cannot understand it or feel He is not answering when we cry out.

"Ron has written this book as the wonderful teacher we have always known him to be, from the perspective of a mature Christian who has lived his Christian life through the most wonderful of times and the most heartbreaking of times. Through it all, Ron has held to his faith in our Lord Jesus.

"As our words reveal, we know the author very closely and love him dearly. When we say we know Ron as a teacher, he was our pastor, and we were youth ministers under his tutelage. But it was more than that. In our early adulthood as Christians, he was our Paul, and we his Timothy.

"When we say he is a mature Christian who throughout his life has experienced the most wonderful of times and the most heartbreaking of times, we know because we were there. We watched as his children grew and matured in the joyful times of life. We were there when his son, Todd, whom he loved very much, as did we, went home to be with our Lord. He was there when our daughter lost her beautiful twin daughters and we, as a father and mother, could not fix it.

"You see, Ron and his loving wife, Judith, have walked this road like Habakkuk and Job and Jeremiah and Peter and Paul and so many others who have gone before, holding to the faith, even when God may seem to be silent. They keep their focus on Jesus and they walk on from the Valley of Despair to the Mountaintop of Praise."

US Representative Mike and Tracy Bost

FOREWORD

"We would not think that the answer to the challenges we all face in life could possibly be found in the book of Habakkuk. In reality, a deeper look at this remarkable prophecy will find the circumstances and solutions for our lives today. Many things change and will change, but some things will always be the same. We will all face disappointment and grief, despair and difficulties, challenges and opposition. Some of those things will be brutal and threaten our lives and attitudes.

Ron Bracy has walked a long and difficult path in his life. Forty-two years in the military, including time in Viet Nam, placed him in dangerous and life-altering moments. His years in military law enforcement and security have exposed him to the worst of evil and violence. He has faced the death of his son, Todd, who died in the military in Albania. In the midst of the grief of their son's death, Ron and Judith lovingly opened their home in St. Louis for their daughter-in-law and grandchildren to live with them until family matters were stabilized. Eventually, both families moved to San Antonio to begin their new lives. Though trained with MDiv and PhD degrees from seminary, he found himself out of work, and even endured being dismissed from a job. Pain, despair, pressing need to find work, and wrestling with his faith were daily companions in his journey. Through many of those things, God seemed to be silent.

"Then his long passion for the book of Habakkuk opened the doors of understanding, faith, and the sufficiency of the Lord. Through the marathon of challenges that were before him, He was able to focus on the Lord and His purposes for his life. From confusion came order and from his desperation came the peace that only God can give. Through it all he gained a deeper understanding of prayer and its strength in his life. God began to reveal to him the divine plan and purpose for all he experienced. While his faith was tested, he never gave up his confidence in God's grace and love. Despite sensing only silence from God, he moved on to discover the exhilaration of praise and fresh fellowship with God. Through it all he walked on!

This is a record of his journey and his triumph over everything that came against him. This is a celebration of the sufficiency of Christ and the sovereignty of God. This is a guide to give you the tools to make your own journey of faith end with strength and confidence. Wherever you are in your journey, you will know that Ron Bracy faced the same things you face and has discovered anew that God is sufficient for every challenge. Read these pages with an open heart and God will establish Himself as the God of grace and mercy found in this volume. You will be blessed and strengthened. So keep on and walk on!"

Dr. Jimmy Draper
President Emeritus, LifeWay

FRODO:
I WISH THE RING HAD NEVER COME TO ME.
I WISH NONE OF THIS HAD HAPPENED.

GANDALF:

SO DO ALL WHO LIVE TO SEE SUCH TIMES.

BUT THAT IS NOT FOR THEM TO DECIDE.

ALL WE HAVE TO DECIDE IS WHAT TO DO

WITH THE TIME THAT IS GIVEN TO US.

J.R.R. TOLKIEN
THE FELLOWSHIP OF THE RING

DEDICATION

TO MY WIFE

Judith, who has patiently traveled this journey with me.

TO MY CHILDREN

Tonya, my first gift from God, and
my runner from the day she was born.

Todd, my second gift from God,
who has completed the journey of life and now has peace.

TO MY GRANDCHILDREN
AND GREAT-GRANDCHILDREN

Thaddeus and his wife, Karina
Taylor
Timothy
Tess
Tate
Tallulah
Isabella
Sofia
Thaddeus Junior

TO MY SON-IN-LAW

David

TO MY DAUGHTER-IN-LAW

Tina

TO MY "HUNDREDFOLD CHILDREN"

All my students at SACS and GSB

TABLE OF CONTENTS

Regardless of the circumstances
and adversities of life,
I could walk on
and know
life had a purpose.

PREFACE

In 1987, I was the pastor of a church in the small town of Murphysboro, Illinois. The editor of the local newspaper asked me to write a series of weekly articles for the religious section of the newspaper. After much thought, I selected the book of Habakkuk as the theme of the articles. I knew the contents of the book dealt with many areas of daily life and would speak to the lives of the readers.

The book of Habakkuk had been a favorite of mine for several years, even predating my attendance at Southwestern Baptist Theological Seminary in Fort Worth, Texas. I had taught the book in various church and home Bible studies in places where I lived. After entering seminary in 1976, where I majored in Old Testament Studies, I began to study the book in more depth and became even more intrigued by its message. At the time my interest was primarily academic, and I approached the book from the perspective of one living in an ivory tower.

It was not that I had not seen the evils and tragedies which exist in this world. I had experienced the deaths of both my parents from long illnesses, but that was just a normal pattern of life. As a combat veteran of Vietnam, I had seen the brutality of war. As an Air Force law enforcement and security officer, I had dealt firsthand with the senselessness of crime. Despite all these experiences, I had merely touched the fringes of evil, pain, and sorrow. In that regard I suspect I was like many people who go through life content and happy, if nothing disturbs their bubble of peace and contentment.

In the years since I wrote those first newspaper articles, the book of Habakkuk moved from the ivory tower to the realities of daily life. Though some details in the many illustrative stories within this book have been modified to protect the identity of individuals and families, the stories are real events which I heard about, participated in, or experienced in my own life. I have seen the iniquity, wickedness, destruction, violence, strife, divisiveness, and injustice which Habakkuk writes about. One truth I have learned through these experiences is that life is never a "rose garden"; the roses have thorns, and those thorns hurt.

Like Habakkuk I have questioned—yes, even challenged—God about His silence and apparent inactivity during the struggles and pains of life. Many times He was silent, and even when He spoke, I could not understand Him. Like the prophet, I learned in time that God is real, active, and at work in my life and the world's. Most of all, I came to understand and acknowledge the truth that God is sovereign (defined as "God's control over all aspects of life"). Only after I accepted His sovereignty did I find and experience the "peace which surpasses all understanding."[1] Regardless of the circumstances and adversities of life, I could walk on and know life had a purpose. All of us eventually must come to this point, if our life is to have true meaning and value.

---

[1]   Philippians 4:7

As you read the pages of this book, I encourage you to seek to understand, acknowledge, and accept God's presence and work in your life. With this truth as our compass, we can be assured that while we may not understand what is happening around and to us, God is still in control. With that assurance, we can trust and obey His commandments and walk in His ways even when the waves of stormy seas threaten to overwhelm us. We can be "people of faith" who wait upon "the appointed vision, because it will not fail; it will certainly come, it will not delay."[2] We can climb through the "Valley of Despair to the Mountaintop of Praise," because "the LORD God is our strength."[3]

In a sermon, Pastor Marianne B. Evett spoke these insightful words about our journey of life and faith, "Most of us are not called upon to be martyrs or prophets. But we are called to be open to the awe and wonder that can bring us to our knees or fill us with tears of joy. You may not be able to make all the glories of the vision last, but in whatever trials that lie ahead, it will sustain you with its promise."[4]

As you read the pages ahead, I pray you will experience God's strength and peace as you travel on your journey of life and faith. Despite your circumstances which may seem to be hopeless, there is hope. In the end, God will enable you to walk on high places!

---

[2] Habakkuk 2:3
[3] Habakkuk 3:19
[4] Marianne Evett, Feast of the Transfiguration. Sermon delivered at All Saints Parish, Brookline, MA, August 4–5, 2007.

Intellectually,
I knew God was there
during all this
"silence of time,"
but I could not hear
His voice.

INTRODUCTION

Yet I will exult in the LORD,
I will rejoice in the God of my salvation.
And, He makes me walk on my high places.
HABAKKUK 3:18, 19C

As I studied Habakkuk and his book and wrote and edited and wrote and edited again and again, I finally reached what I thought was the final stage of mailing the manuscript of *Walk On* to a publisher. *How little did I know of God and His workings!* As a civilian, I attended seminary for twelve years and completed both a master's and PhD degrees. I taught as an adjunct professor in colleges and graduate schools for several years, and had been a pastor for twenty-five years. *How little did I know of God and His workings!* As a career military officer from my first day as a cadet at the Air Force Academy until my retirement, I served forty-two years in the United States Air Force. I flew 183 combat missions as a WSO in the RF-4C during the Vietnam War, and I was on duty at the Pentagon on 9/11 and lived through that tragic event. I also served twenty years as a military chaplain and was deployed throughout the world to many hot spots. *How little did I know of God and His workings!*

On April 1, 2005, I began a journey of life and faith that I had never walked. I came face-to-face with God in a way I had never envisioned. I had dealt with death many times throughout my military and civilian life, but it had always been from a third-person perspective. Except for the deaths of my mother and father—and they had died in the normal process of life from long illnesses—I had not been personally involved in the many deaths I had experienced. I was either the chaplain or the pastor who ministered to the families of the dead person.

That all changed with a telephone call at 12:24 a.m., April 1, 2005. As I listened to the words of my daughter-in-law, her anguish and pain crossing the thousands of miles from England to St. Louis, my mind struggled to wake up and grasp their meaning. My blood chilled as she sobbed brokenly, inconsolably: "Dad, Todd is *missing*! He was on a mission, and contact was lost with his plane at 8:05 p.m. last night [March 31, 2005]. There is some information in Albanian newspapers, but nothing is certain. Can you and Mom come to England? I need you! The girls need you!" In the short span of time which those few words took, my life and my family's lives changed forever. *I was to learn much about sorrow, hope, and God!*

After hanging up from the call, I shared the conversation with Judith, my wife. Both of us were in tears as I went to the computer and began a search of the Internet to see if there was any further information. It took about five minutes, and I was looking at the wreckage of my son's plane on the front page of an Albanian newspaper. The article was sketchy, but in my military career I had witnessed such scenes numerous times. My heart and mind knew what search and rescue teams would later confirm—my son was dead! Time *stopped* for me!

The events which played out in the days, weeks, and months afterwards, from April to mid-August—two memorial services in England; two funerals at Arlington National Cemetery in Washington, DC; one household move from England to St. Louis, as our daughter-in-law and two granddaughters moved in with us; then, two household moves, as we all moved from St. Louis to San Antonio—these all transpired in a silence of time. To this day, the memories of those four and one half months are mere shadows. I lived and functioned out of habit and instinct. My mind was numb, and my heart beat only to pump blood. There was no feeling, just pain and emptiness!

Intellectually, I knew God was there during all this "silence of time," but I could not hear His voice. Like Habakkuk, I cried out over and over, "How long, O LORD, will I call for help, and Thou will not hear?"[5] Silence filled my mind and heart. Nor could I hear the voices of the many people who attended the memorial and funeral services, or came to visit and help us. I resigned as pastor of the church in St. Louis, where I had served since retirement from the military, and Judith resigned her job with Curves Fitness. We left behind friends and family (our daughter and her family) and moved to San Antonio to rebuild our lives, but there was only silence. Time had lost all meaning for me. My son was dead, and in many respects, so was I!

For the first six months we lived in San Antonio, I could not find

---

[5]   Habakkuk 1:2

a job. In seminary, I had obtained a PhD with the hope of teaching, but I soon realized that a PhD was not a magic key to a teaching position. With nothing to do, I went back to school. The only reason was to keep my mind busy, to shut out the silence which filled me. I entered a high school teacher's certification program at a local college. The courses were engaging and enlightening, the professors were challenging, and my fellow students were encouraging. I completed the courses in a year and passed the Texas State Teacher Certification Exam, but I could not find a teaching position. Even worse, the silence still surrounded me.

After six months I was hired at USAA headquarters in San Antonio, which at least filled some of the silence. After two years an opportunity for advancement in position and salary occurred, and I moved to a regional communications company. The money was good, but what I saw in how people lived and thought was not who I was. Those four years in the business world convinced me I was not a corporate person. On April 16, 2010, I left Spectrum Fitness Center to drive to work. As I walked to my Jeep—which had been my son's—I simply looked up to the heavens and said, "God, I don't care what You do or how You do it, just get me out of this desert!" And he did!

At 5:00 p.m. that afternoon I walked out the doors of the communications company with a pink slip in my hand. As I walked down the steps, I raised my arms in a Rocky Balboa-like victory salute and said, "Thank You, God!" Though I had no job, a calm assurance and peace filled my heart. I sensed I would be teaching before the summer was over. A crack had appeared in the shell of silence ... though it was only a small crack, barely perceptible, I had heard the still, small voice of God. I knew He was there with me, and He was no longer silent.

The next four months were the calmest days I had experienced in the nearly five years since Todd's death. Even as the days of summer ended, and no teaching position had opened for me, I still believed I would be teaching before the summer was over. In the last week of July, less than three weeks before school would start in San Antonio, I received a telephone call from a local private Christian school. At Judith's insistence, I had sent a resume to the school only the week before. The person on the telephone identified himself as the principal of the high school and asked if I would be interested in an interview with the school superintendent. The high school was looking for a Bible teacher, and he and the superintendent believed I might fit the bill. Ironically, the principal himself was leaving the school the next week for another school, but he encouraged me to consider the interview. He did not have to ask me twice. In a strange way, I knew God was speaking, just as He had in April when He took me out of the corporate world.

One week and two interviews later, first with the superintendent and then with the new high school principal, I was offered a position as the sophomore Bible teacher at San Antonio Christian High School. It was less than two weeks before the teachers' in-service training began for the new school year. Tears flowed down my face when I was offered the position. Little did I know God had a lot more to say to me in the days, months, and years ahead! As

He had with Habakkuk, God said, "I am going to do something in your days that you will not believe."[6] He has over and over!

Although I was a newbie as a high school teacher, my colleagues, the administrators, the parents, and the students accepted me with open arms and hearts. At last I was home, and God's shell of silence had disappeared. This became clear one class period in mid-November that first year. As an introduction to Christian Philosophy, I had been leading the students in a study of the biblical Daniel, a teenager himself. I was showing the class how Daniel had been torn away from everything precious in his life—family, friends, home, temple, city, country—and was now living in a country and culture foreign to his way of life and thinking. He had lost everything!

As an illustration, I pointed out to the class how Jesus brought the apostle Peter face-to-face with this same truth. After Jesus explained the Parable of the Rich Young Ruler to the disciples, Peter remarked, "We have left everything to follow You." I then read aloud the following words of Jesus: "I tell you the truth, no one who has left home or brothers or sisters or mother or father or children or fields for me and the gospel will fail to receive a hundred times as much in this present age—homes, brothers, sisters, mothers, children and fields."[7] As I uttered the last words of the verse, I stood there in silence, my heart frozen, my mind whirling. The students sat quietly, aware that something was going on within their teacher.

---

6   Habakkuk 1:5
7   Mark 10:17–27

Like a lightning bolt, it hit me: I, too, had lost everything—home, family, friends, jobs, and my son. God had taken Todd—my only son—but in his place, He had given me children "a hundred times as much." I had 107 sophomore students that first year at SACS. In that moment, I came alive. There was no more silence. God had spoken!

With tears flowing, I shared what God had said to me, and I literally embraced my students that day. From that day until now—and I know it will forever be the case—my students are not just students; they are my children. Each year since that first year, God has given me a new class of students as my children. Every year, I share the story of "a hundred times" with my new classes. They need to know that in all circumstances, good and bad, God is always with us; He is not silent; and, most of all, He is sovereign! Despite where we are on the journey of life and faith, God will take us through the Valley of Despair to the Mountaintop of Praise.

It has been hard to complete this manuscript, but God has been faithful. He has opened my mind and my heart to what He wants me to write, and there has been a new freedom to express my feelings.

Todd's favorite music group was U2. Before his death, I had not paid much attention to their music, but afterwards I started to listen to them as one way of remembering my son. I even bought a couple of biographies and discovered the spiritual background of their lives and music. One of U2's songs is entitled "Walk On." Its message of pain and brokenness, and the necessity to endure and walk on regardless of the circumstances spoke to my heart.[8] How true are those words for us to hear. They are the words of Habakkuk!

All who have experienced the death of a loved one know the pain and emptiness it causes. Unlike what well-meaning people say in their efforts to offer comfort, time does not heal the heart. The pain and emptiness does not magically disappear at the end of two or three or five years. The artist who designed the jewelry of a heart with a hole in it was right on track. My heart will always have a hole in it, and nothing in this world will ever fill that hole.

As I have walked on this pain-filled journey, I have learned so much about this awesome God we worship. Like Habakkuk, I thought God had forsaken me. The words of Jesus as He hung on the cross resonated in my heart: "My God, My God, why hast Thou forsaken Me?"[9] For many a dark night, God did not perform any miracles of healing in my life. He did not take away the pain. He did not fill the emptiness. He did not answer my "whys."

During this journey from the Valley of Despair to the Mountaintop of Praise, God taught me many lessons. I discovered God is not silent: even in His silence, He spoke to my heart. When He seemed so far away, He was close to me. When He did not work a miracle, and restore my son to life as He did with the son of the widow of Nain, He worked in my life. When the days were dark and the nights were lonely, He gave me strength to walk on! As He did with the Israelites in the wilderness when He gave them the exact amount of manna

---

8   U2. "Walk On," in *All That You Can't Leave Behind,* Island/Inter Scope Records, 2001, CD.
9   Matthew 27:46

they needed for each day, God has done for me. As I look back over the years since Todd's death, I can see how God has given me manna each day to deal with the experiences of life. That has been His healing miracle in my life. With Habakkuk, I can "walk on my high places" with God as my strength.

I do not know where you are in your journey of life and faith. Perhaps you have never walked with God in your life; you have doubted His reality. Perhaps you have experienced some great tragedy, and you cannot understand why a loving God would allow such pain. Perhaps you have looked at a world filled with evil and injustice and asked, "Why, God?"

I encourage you to continue to walk on. As He did in my life, God will meet you in His time and show you how He wants to walk with you on your journey of life and faith.

May you, too, experience His presence, guidance, and providence on your journey from the Valley of Despair to the Mountaintop of Praise. Along the way, always remember, "God is sovereign! He is in control, and He will always be with you!" *Walk on!!!*

*Why did God
let this happen?*

CHAPTER ONE
THE BURDEN OF PAIN

The burden which Habakkuk
the prophet saw.
How long, O LORD,
will I call for help and
Thou wilt not hear?
I cry out to Thee,
'Violence!'
yet Thou dost not save.

HABAKKUK 1:1–2

"Oh, God! No! No! No!" the young mother wailed as she knelt over the broken body of her four-year-old daughter. Moments before, the small, beautiful brunette girl was laughing and shouting as she rode her new tricycle on the sidewalk in front of their suburban home. In one terrifying endless moment, a drunk driver had sped around the corner, lost control of his car, and run into the child. Her body lay crumbled on the sidewalk, and the onlooking neighbors and friends stood stunned as they gazed helplessly at the scene. The tragedy was mind-numbing! Later, as the EMT medics carefully loaded the gurney with the dead body of the girl into the ambulance, the young mother looked up into her pastor's face, and with tears running down her face, cried out in anger: "Why, Pastor? Why? Why did God let this happen?"

"Pastor, it's not *fair*! I needed her so much! Why did God take her now?"

For nearly a year the husband had watched his wife of twelve years, the mother of their three young children, die slowly and painfully from an unknown type of cancer. The evening before, she had died quietly in her sleep. Now, the man, who for years had been a tower of strength in the local community church, was shattered—physically, emotionally, and spiritually. What words of comfort could the pastor, a newlywed of only three months, offer to this brokenhearted man?

"Senseless! Why, God?" Standing at the grave of the young college student, the pastor considered the faces of the boy's parents. Other family members and friends milled around the grave, and the same shocked look filled their faces. Five days of agony had passed since the young man disappeared without a trace. Hours of waiting had stretched on endlessly as the parents prayed and hoped while police, friends, and neighbors searched for any clue to his whereabouts. The pastor himself had flown a couple of search missions in a Cessna 152, hoping to find some trace of the missing boy. All to no avail. It was as if the ground had opened and swallowed the boy: no trace could be found of him anywhere. Then, on the sixth morning, as the Sunday worship services ended, the news came, and all their hopes were shattered. His body had been found.

"God, was this necessary?" the pastor thought. As a veteran of the Vietnam War, he had faced death many times. Friends and comrades had died in the long war, but they were soldiers and had fought and died for a cause. This death was so senseless and needless. How could he answer the parent's and parishioners' questions and ease their sorrow? Why did God allow such a brutal murder to happen?

The little boy, grasping his grandmother's hand tightly, looked up at the pastor and softly said: "Why did God take Mommy and Daddy to heaven? Doesn't He have enough people to play with? I don't have *anyone* to play with now." Silently, the pastor turned away to hide the tears which filled his eyes. He said nothing;

there was nothing he could say.

The woman sat sobbing. The bitterness and pain was visible in her body. The pastor had been studying for next Sunday's sermon when his secretary had come into the study and said, "Pastor, there is a young woman who is begging to see you. She doesn't have an appointment, and I know you are busy, but I believe you may want to talk with her." Knowing that ministry was about people and not sermons, the pastor told the secretary to bring the woman in. Now he sat quietly listening as she poured out her story of betrayal and despair.

"Pastor, how could he do it? How could he walk out on me and the children? How could he leave us for another woman, my best friend? He says he wants a divorce. What am I supposed to do? I don't have a job, and I don't have any family here to help me. How could God let this happen?

Like a continuous digital loop, such events play over and over in every pastor's life and ministry. The questions are always the same; only the names of the people change. Every pastor, from the newest ministerial student who has just graduated from seminary to the seasoned veteran with years of ministry, is confronted with the same age-old questions. Why does evil exist? Why does God allow injustice? What is the purpose of pain and suffering? How is a person supposed to deal with the grief and agony which fills the soul when a beloved family member or close friend dies? What is a person to do in times of despair? How is the person to travel the journey of life and faith when all the familiar ways are hidden in the fog of grief?

No one has all the answers to these tough questions. Though God provides some answers in the Bible for times of sorrow, we must walk on in the sorrow. While He shows us some light during periods of darkness, we must walk on in the darkness. Though He grants us some peace of mind during the storms of life and faith, we must step out and walk on through the stormy winds.

One of the clearest accounts in which God provides insight into the issue of despair is found in the Hebrew Old Testament book of Habakkuk. The text records the personal and traumatic experiences the prophet Habakkuk encountered with evil, injustice, grief, and despair. In extremely blunt language, Habakkuk questions God, much like a prosecuting attorney questions a defendant. The prophet could not understand why God was silent during terrible evil and injustice. Habakkuk, like us, wanted answers!

From the prophet's experience with God, we can glean certain truths that will empower us to deal with evil and grief along the journey of life and faith. These truths will provide an anchor and enable us to stand firm during the storms of life and faith. The truths are not easy, and God does not promise us an easy journey. Though our life may be filled with confusion and doubts, God is sovereign, He in control, and He will never leave us. That is all that we need to know!

In the pages ahead let us travel together the path Habakkuk set before us. Let us walk on from the Valley of Despair to the Mountaintop of Praise. The journey is long, winding, and demanding, but at the end, you will find as Habakkuk did, and as I did, that you will walk on high places.

REFLECTIONS

1. Have you experienced a tragic loss in your life such as those described in this chapter?

2. How have you responded to this loss?

3. What are the unanswered questions which fill your thoughts?

4. What answers have you found for your questions?

CHAPTER TWO
WALKING INTO
THE VALLEY OF DESPAIR

How long, O LORD, will I call for help,
And Thou will not hear?
I cry out to Thee, 'Violence!'
Yet Thou dost not save.
Why dost Thou make me see iniquity,
And cause me to look on wickedness?
Yes, destruction and violence are before me;
Strife exists and contention arises.

Therefore, the law is ignored
And justice is never upheld.
For the wicked surround the righteous;
Therefore, justice comes out perverted. "
[God replied,] "Look among the nations!
Observe! Be astonished! Wonder!
Because I am doing something in your days—
You would not believe if you were told.
For behold, I am raising up the Chaldeans.

HABAKKUK 1:2–6
[Brackets mine]

At Southwestern Baptist Theological Seminary in Fort Worth, Texas, there is a story about a young preacher boy's traumatic entry into the Valley of Despair. Some say the story is true; others think it is merely a myth. The truth probably lies somewhere in between. For certain, the Valley of Despair is familiar to many of us.

First-period classes at the seminary start at 8:00 a.m. every Tuesday through Friday. No classes are held on Mondays so that the students can travel back to the seminary from the many towns and villages where they preach on Sundays. One Tuesday morning, during the second month of the fall semester, one of the students casually walked into his first period Greek class and sat down in his seat in the last row on the left side of the room. He had missed class the previous Friday because of a revival meeting he had preached in a rural Panhandle Texas village over the weekend. He did not know the Greek professor had announced at the end of class on Friday that there would be a test Tuesday morning. Unaware of the impending test, the student opened his textbook, dug a pencil out of his backpack, took a notebook out, and prepared to take lecture notes.

Idly, he gazed outside at the beautiful fall day through the floor-to-ceiling windows which lined the outer wall of the classroom. Puffy white clouds floated across the icy blue sky. The leaves on the countless huge old pecan trees that dotted the campus lawns swayed in a gentle breeze. Several squirrels chattered nosily as they ran across the ground, seeking pecans that had fallen from the trees. He could see students' wives wandering through the trees as they gathered pecans to take home to make pies and candy for their families. This was just one of the many ways the wives supplemented their families' meager food budgets. The student's mind was not focused on what was going on in the classroom.

As was his custom, the Greek professor called upon one of the students to open the class with prayer. After a few minutes of offering praises and thanksgiving to God for the blessings of the past weekend and passionate petitions for strength and protection, the student fervently said: "And, Lord, help us have clear minds as we take our test this morning."

That was as far as he got. From the back of the room, another voice blurted out loud enough to be heard upstairs in the dean's office: "Test? *What* test?" Shocked, everyone turned to stare. Sitting upright and rigid in his chair, the student sat with a glazed sick look on his face. Suddenly, and without any warning, he had been thrown into a Valley of Despair.

Within this story lies an important principle of life: *we never know when some unexpected circumstance of life will confront us and test our faith.* Daily, we fool ourselves. We arrogantly think we have all the answers to life and can control whatever happens to us. We mistakenly believe if we ignore the unpleasant events which continually occur in the world around us, we will not be affected. We are only concerned about our personal contentment. Like the ancient Hebrew King Hezekiah, who was warned by the prophet Isaiah of impending dangers, we think, "There will be peace and truth in my days."[10]

Yet without warning and out of a clear blue sky, a dark violent storm swirls across our path, thunder shatters the silence with loud blasts like giant cannons, and spears of brilliant lightning flash across the black sky now filled with rolling angry clouds. Our peaceful and comfortable world is suddenly shattered. Our age-long traditions, soothing rituals, established doctrines, and pat answers are not so certain anymore. Our confidence, like a sand castle battered by the rising tide, crumbles beneath an onslaught of frightening doubts.

We cry out, "Test? What test?" We want answers, but none of the answers satisfy us or bring peace to our troubled hearts. Nor do the soothing platitudes other people offer us take away the hurt which lies deep within our souls. Fear threatens to engulf us. Our world becomes dark. The walls close in. Despair overwhelms us. We are alone, or so it seems. Like the young student, we find ourselves staggering through a Valley of Despair.

Welcome to the world of Habakkuk, an ancient Hebrew prophet. Welcome to his world in which everything seemed

---

[10] Isaiah 39:8

to be topsy-turvy: a world of injustice and evil, violence and sorrow. A world in which it seemed as if there was no God. Even if God existed, He did not appear to care what happened to the "good" people. Understand: this is not only Habakkuk's world, it is our world as well.

Habakkuk lived in or near the ancient city of Jerusalem around 600 BC While there is some evidence of a general time frame for the prophet's life and ministry, scholars are not certain of the specific time when the prophet lived and wrote. For a lengthy period, Habakkuk had witnessed grave injustice, evil, pain, and suffering, and he had cried out to God for answers numerous times. But God had not answered! Finally, after many cries and an unknown period, God replied. Through the prophet's recorded words from God, we can learn many lessons of life and faith.

First, in response to the prophet's questions about God's inactivity,[11] God replied, "[Habakkuk], I am raising up the Chaldeans, that fierce and impetuous people who march throughout the earth."[12] God was at work! The name "Chaldeans" is another term for the fierce warrior peoples known as the Babylonians, who ruled the Ancient Middle East from 609 to 539 BC. The prophet knew these Chaldeans; he knew they were evil!

Second, we can further narrow the time of Habakkuk's ministry based on God's warning of impending judgment on Judah for their evil disobedience.[13] God was going to allow the Chaldeans/ Babylonians to conquer and destroy Judah. History, both biblical

[11] Habakkuk 1:1–4
[12] Habakkuk 1:6
[13] Habakkuk 1:12

and extra-biblical, records the occurrence of this event in 587 BC[14] We can date Habakkuk's life and ministry sometime during the time frame of 609 BC and 587 BC. Following the destruction of Jerusalem, we do not know anything definite about Habakkuk, except he may have been a singer in the Temple choir.[15]

One thing set Habakkuk apart from the other Old Testament prophets. He was not a messenger from God to the people; instead, he was a messenger from the people to God. The prophet boldly and stridently challenged God as he sought answers to issues which confronted him daily. As we read his words, we can sense—and empathize with—the troubled spirit of Habakkuk.

"The burden which Habakkuk the prophet saw."[16] These opening words of the book reveal the prophet was deeply concerned about the violent and evil circumstances that surrounded him. The book is personal and experiential. It is not written from or for some idealistic utopian world. Instead the book records a dialogue between Habakkuk and God in which the prophet is confused, angry, and bitter. He is hurting emotionally, psychologically, and spiritually. God is hidden and silent: evil, pain, and suffering fills the prophet's world.

The prophet was not content with the answers his traditional Jewish faith offered. He wanted real answers with meaning in a real world. Out of his despair, Habakkuk dared to ask God what some might call forbidden questions, such as: "God, if You are good and all-powerful, why do You allow evil to exist?" "If You

---

[14] 2 Kings 22–25
[15] Habakkuk 3:20
[16] Habakkuk 1:1

are all-knowing, why do You not answer my prayers and help me understand your plan for Your chosen people and for me?" "If You are everywhere, why can I not find You?" Questions which are familiar to us!

The text also makes it clear that this situation had extended over a lengthy period: "How long, O LORD, will I call for help and Thou wilt not hear?"[17] Tension as taut as a strung bowstring vibrates from the pages. The book makes many of us uneasy about our faith. The dialogue of the prophet is not just some scroll from the past. It is true to life, and the prophet's message is of great value for our modern, fast-paced world. The questions of the prophet are the same questions that fill our hearts, confound our minds, and pour out of our mouths two and a half millennia later. We experience the same feelings of despair in our own heart.

Like the prophet, our life often does not match our beliefs. Silence about the hard issues of life pervades most people's lives. This silence is expressed by the wide toothy smile and the words, "Oh, I'm fine" whenever anyone asks how we are doing. Even when our world is crumbling, pride keeps us from facing or speaking the truth. How desperately we need to learn from the prophet!

Through his words the prophet records his own journey of life and faith through the Valley of Despair to the Mountaintop of Praise. It is a journey many biblical people have traveled: Abraham, Joseph, Hannah, Ruth, Elijah, Job, Mary, and even Jesus Christ. Throughout subsequent centuries, countless others have traveled this very road, and they invite us to join them on this

---

[17]   Habakkuk 1:2

journey of life and faith. As the unknown writer of the New Testament book of Hebrews proclaimed: "Therefore, since we have so great a cloud of witnesses surrounding us, let us also lay aside every encumbrance, and the sin which so easily entangles us, and let us run with endurance the race that is set before us."[18]

Like a road map, the book of Habakkuk provides guidance as we travel this journey of life and faith. Through his experience, the prophet exemplifies how to live through a period of suffering and emerge from the dark Valley of Despair with our faith intact and stronger. There are dangers we must be aware of lest we fall. Like road signs on a meandering mountain road, several warning signs alert us to the dangers ahead.

First, *the journey is not short.* It is not a commuter flight that is over in less than an hour. The journey may be a lifelong one that ends only at the grave. The race of life is not a hundred-yard sprint; it is a marathon. Only those who persevere will reach the finish line. The apostle Paul spoke of this need for perseverance in his last book. Writing to Timothy, his son in the Christian faith, Paul encouraged the young man to endure and continue in the truths and ways of the faith that the apostle had taught him. Paul's triumphant words were a model for Timothy to follow and still echo for us today: "I have fought the good fight, I have finished the course, and I have kept the faith."[19] Paul understood the journey of life is not short. We must have the same attitude and spirit!

Second, *the journey is not easy*: the obstacles are many and dif-

---

[18]   Hebrews 12:1
[19]   2 Timothy 4:7

ficult, and the directions are often unclear. The difficulties of the journey challenge a person's faith, and people generally respond in one of two ways. Some become bitter, skeptical, and turn away from God. Others turn to God, and, despite the difficulties, renew and strengthen their faith. Jesus, the apostle John, and the writer of the book of Hebrews all allude to the necessity of perseverance until the race of life is finished.[20]

Finally, *no one has an absolute single answer which will resolve this demanding journey for someone else.* Many books have been written, many lectures have been presented, and many videos have been shown, but they only offer words of encouragement, not absolute answers. As an individual travels the journey of life, he or she must find his or her own answers. The book of Habakkuk offers several lessons of life for us to consider.

First, Habakkuk teaches that *difficulties and tragedies are going to occur in our lives.* In other words, God does not promise us a rosebush without thorns. Many people, even Christians, deny this truth. I have several rosebushes in my yard, and the most amazing thing happens every time I prune them—I always get pricked by a thorn, resulting in pain.

This denial started when we were children. Remember the fairy tales our parents read to us each night as they tucked us into bed? The courageous prince saved the beautiful princess from the wicked witch or fiery dragon. The prince carried the princess away on his swift white stallion to his magnificent castle, and they "lived happily ever after."

---

[20] Matthew 24:10–13; 1 John 2:19; Hebrews 10:37–39

As adults, we hear similar fairy tales. From various platforms, religious leaders proclaim a simple message: "If a person will only accept Jesus Christ, everything will be all right." Prosperity theology—"health, wealth, and welfare"—fills the bookshelves of Christian bookstores and resounds in church sanctuaries and across the airwaves of television. There is one small glitch—the Bible does not teach this modern-day fairy tale! Remember, Jesus warned His disciples: "In this world you will have tribulation."[21]

A similar message is proclaimed in the secular world. Psychologists, counselors, and self-improvement gurus of all persuasions offer countless self-help videos and books. Infomercials advertise simple seven- or ten- or twelve-step programs to resolve all adversities. Despite all efforts to deny the truth, difficulties and tragedies are a part of our lives in this world.

As Habakkuk looked around his world, all he could see was evil: bloodshed and violence filled the land. History reveals that the last twenty-five years of the nation of Judah were wrought with evil. The four kings who ruled during this period were godless and greedy men who used their power to oppress the nation. Slave-like conditions existed as citizens were forced into various building projects. Taxes consumed economic resources. Bribery filled the judges' hands, and justice was twisted and meaningless.

No wonder the prophet cried out, "How long, O LORD, will I call for help and Thou wilt not hear?"[22] Habakkuk was baffled because God did not reply. This did not match the prophet's theol-

---

21   John 16:33
22   Habakkuk 1:2

ogy. Was this just the world of Habakkuk? No, it is also our world!

We, too, inhabit the same world of evil: pain and sorrow, toil and trouble, bloodshed and violence. We read it in the daily newspapers or on the Internet. We turn on our TVs, and it invades our homes. There are no sanctuaries for us. Like the ancient prophet, we cry out, "God, why? Why do You allow this to happen? Why don't You use Your power and stop this evil? Why are You so silent and faraway? Do You even exist?" Like Habakkuk, we find ourselves in the Valley of Despair. There seems to be no answers!

In his book *The Tracks of a Fellow Struggler*, Reverend John Claypool relates an incident out of his own Valley of Despair. During his ten-year-old daughter's struggle with leukemia which ended in her death one year later, the little girl looked up one day from her hospital bed and said, "Daddy, have you prayed to God about when my pain is going to stop? Have you asked God when He is going to bring this to an end?" Brokenhearted, he replied, "Yes, honey, I have prayed." With tears trickling down her small cheeks, the little girl asked, "Well, what did He say?" With his head hung in agony, Claypool sat by her side and said nothing, because God had said nothing to him![23]

This divine silence causes many people to doubt the power and love of God. British philosopher Bertrand Russell, in his lecture "Why I Am Not a Christian," states one of the reasons he is not a Christian is that he could not accept a loving God who would

---

[23]   John Claypool, *The Tracks of a Fellow Struggler* (New York: Church Publishing Inc., 2004), 77.

allow suffering and evil to exist.[24] Like Habakkuk, Claypool, and Russell, we want answers to our problems in life—and we want the answers right now!

This creates another problem. We already know what we want the answers to be. We want God to work in a certain way, to answer us in a specific way. When we do not receive the expected answer, we experience more despair. Caught in a whirlpool of emotions, we are dragged deeper and deeper until we are lost in the darkness of doubt.

A second truth we learn from the prophet is that *God is not silent.* After an indefinite period, God spoke: "Habakkuk, look among the nations! Observe! Be astonished! Because I AM doing something in your days." In other words, God says: "Habakkuk, open your eyes! I am here, I am in control, and I am still at work in your world." This is our problem. Like the prophet, we are so focused on our problems we do not see God at work around us. The ancient psalmist wrote, "The heavens declare the glory of God; the skies proclaim the work of His hands. Day after day they pour forth speech; and night after night they display knowledge. There is no speech or language where their voice is not heard. Their voice goes out into all the earth; their words to the end of the world."[25]

Stop! Take a moment! Reflect! Observe the greatness of the universe that surrounds us: the warmth of the sun, the light of the moon, the myriad of stars at night. Compare the delicacy of the

---

[24]   Bertrand Russell, *Why I Am Not a Christian and Other Essays on Religion and Related Subjects,* Ed. Paul Edwards (New York: Simon and Schuster, 1967), 3–23.
[25]   Psalm 19:1–4

beautiful tiny bluebonnet flower and the overwhelming majestic grandeur of the Grand Canyon. Listen to the gentle whispering wind of the giant redwoods and the awesome roar of Niagara Falls. "Be still and know that God is God."[26] Francis Schaeffer, author of *He Is There and He Is Not Silent*, concludes that modern man's denial of the existence of God creates an unanswerable dilemma. "Man's damnation today is that he can find no meaning for man. He is lost. Man remains a zero." Schaeffer goes on to say that "without the infinite-personal God ... there is no answer to the existence of what exists ... The answer to the problem of existence is that the infinite-personal, triune God is there ... and He is not silent."[27] Job, Isaiah, and Habakkuk all learned this.[28] We must learn it too!

Habakkuk states another truth: "*God is not powerless.*" Neither the evil kings of Judah, nor the ruthless Babylonians could thwart the purposes of God. History reveals the truth of God's words. "My word which goes forth from My mouth shall not return to me empty without accomplishing what I desire, and without succeeding in the matter for which I sent it."[29] In His own time God brought justice to Habakkuk's world. In His own time God will bring justice to our world.

The power of God is taught throughout the Bible. One such story is of Jesus and His disciples caught in a great storm on the Sea of Galilee. While Jesus sleeps, the disciples struggle to keep the

---

[26] Psalm 46:10
[27] Frances Schaeffer, *He Is There, and He Is Not Silent* (Wheaton, IL: Tyndale House Publishers, 1972), 11–18.
[28] Job 42; Isaiah 6; Habakkuk 1
[29] Isaiah 55:11

boat from sinking. In despair the disciples awaken Jesus and cry out, "Master! Master! Save us; we are perishing!" Standing up, Jesus looked at the raging wind and waves and said, "Peace be still!" Instantly, the storm ceased and the seas became perfectly calm. Jesus looked at the disciples and said, "Why are you timid, you men of little faith?" Awed, the disciples murmur, "Who then is this? He commands the winds and the water, and they obey Him!"[30]

We are astonished at the seeming lack of compassion of Jesus. How could He be so callous and call His disciples "men of little faith?" The answer lies not in the immediate circumstances, but in what Jesus had said to them earlier—words which they had forgotten during the storm. Before they left the shore to cross the sea, Jesus said: "Let us go over to the other side."[31] He did not say, "Let us go out into the middle of the sea and sink!"

The same is true today. As God said to Habakkuk, and as Jesus said to the disciples: "Open your eyes and look around you. I AM here, and I AM in control. I will not let you sink!"

In the years 1998 to 2000, I experienced one of the darkest storms in all my years as a pastor.

In fall 1998, I resigned from a church in Illinois where I had been pastor for seven and a half years. My wife and I moved far away from our family and friends as I took a new pastoral position at a church in Montana. A year earlier the church had experienced a split which left it with about one-third of its original membership. A former mentor contacted me and asked if I would consider

---

30   Matthew 8:23–27; Mark 4:35–41; Luke 8:22–25
31   Mark 4:35

coming to the church as pastor. After much prayer, Judith and I both sensed God leading us to make the move and believed we could help the congregation recover from its deep hurt. We were excited about the new opportunity and challenge.

In the early days of the pastorate, the church began to grow as the Lord brought new people into the church. Most of them were young adults who were non-believers or who had been out of church for many years. Several instances occurred where entire families were redeemed by Jesus and baptized into the fellowship of the church. A joyous spirit filled the worship services; God was obviously at work.

Everything seemed fine during the first nine months, but small disturbing incidents soon began to occur. One member, who had been a member of several other churches in the town, became disgruntled when changes were made in the administrative structure of the church. He began to disrupt every business session over anything and everything that was discussed. One time the man even had to be restrained when he became extremely vitriolic. A couple of other members verbally attacked the music minister, who also served as the youth minister. Other members began to spread gossip and rumors. A critical spirit began to grow among the older members who had remained in the church after the earlier split. One by one, some men stopped attending a morning coffee gathering. When asked why, they said they did not want to be with some of the other men who always made negative critical comments. I and other church leaders made numerous personal visits to the people who were creating the conflict. All efforts of resolution and reconciliation were rebuffed. Nothing stopped the vicious circle of criticism.

During this time, one church leader was discovered to be involved in pornography. He rejected any help and refused to step down from his leadership positions. In the end, church discipline had to be taken, and that seemed to be the final straw. The critical elements began to take secret steps—they thought—to get rid of me as pastor of the church.

All this occurred over a span of a year during which I continually prayed, "How long, O Lord? How long will I call for help, and You do not hear?" As the critical spirit slowly engulfed the church, families who joined the church in those first nine months became discouraged and withdrew from church activities. Some left the church. When encouraged to stay to help resolve the situation, they said, "Pastor, we are not leaving because of you. We cannot worship God with these people and their critical spirit."

During these dark days, I sought advice from several denominational leaders whom I trusted. They encouraged me to continue in my duties as pastor, but I could not find peace. The daily attacks by the disgruntled clique began to take a toll on my wife and me. In the end, I resigned from the church in October 2000. I did not want to be a hindrance to whatever God chose to do. Several years later I learned God—in His own way and in His own time—disciplined those who had created the spirit of criticism in His church. God is neither powerless nor silent!

In those dark and lonesome days when God seemed to be silent,

He was already at work on my behalf. The local associational director of missions led the church membership—despite opposition by the critical clique—to allocate for us a substantial sum of money equal to six months of salary and moving expenses. A friend from another church was a real estate agent, and he worked to sell our house which we had owned for only a year. Astonishingly, the house sold for cash on the last day of the year during winter! The real estate agent even refused to take a commission.

There was one condition to the sale: Judith and I had to be out of the house in nine days. That was a huge challenge, but God was not absent nor silent: He was at work. Friends and members of the church flocked to our house and helped pack our possessions and load the countless boxes and furniture onto two moving trucks. They even provided the boxes. One member of the church, volunteered to take off from his job and drive one of the trucks to Omaha, Nebraska, where our son lived. On January 10, 2001, on God's appointed timetable, we drove away from our former house and headed to Illinois. As mile after mile passed, the darkness of those two years of struggle drifted away as God began to erase the hurt and pain.

Several challenges still faced us. Judith and I had no place to live in Illinois, and I did not have a job. Remember, God does not take us out into the middle of a lake and let us sink. He is always at work! In Omaha, the church member (our driver) returned home to Montana, and our son took leave from the military and drove the second truck the rest of the way to Illinois. Even as we crossed the plains of the Midwest, God provided a house for us in Murphysboro, Illinois, about five minutes from where our daughter lived.

On January 17, 2001, we reached Murphysboro, Illinois, and three days later we were settled in our new home. For the next month and a half, I looked for a job and applied to several law schools. Before leaving Montana, I had taken the law school applicant test. Two law schools accepted my applications, so I began to prepare to go to law school.

Everything seemed to be settled for us, but God was not finished; He was still at work! On February 20, I received a call from my Air National Guard Wing in Montana. The Wing personnel officer asked if I would be interested in a special assignment to the Pentagon. She explained what the assignment would be, and although the duties were outside my specialty, I quickly responded, "Yes." She told me I would receive a call from the Pentagon in a few days.

On February 25, the colonel in charge of the special assignment at the Pentagon called. He interviewed me over the telephone for nearly an hour. Before he hung up, he said another person would call me for a second interview. The very next day I received a second call from the Pentagon, this time from the colonel who would be my supervisor. She also questioned me in detail. At the end of the conversation, she said she wanted me to come to the Pentagon and work for her, adding that orders were being cut to recall me to active duty. I would be relieved from my unit in Montana and reassigned to the Pentagon. On March 15, 2001, I reported for active duty in J6 Division of the Joint Chiefs of Staff and served there until March 20, 2002. When God works, He can work quickly!

The vital lesson I re-learned through the events of 1998 to 2001 was that even in the darkest of times when faced with seemingly overwhelming obstacles, God is sovereign, and He is in control. God is not silent; we simply must learn to hear His voice. God is at work in our lives; we must open our eyes to see how and where He is working. We must not lean on our own understanding; we must trust in God's promises, wait on His timetable, obey His words, and follow His ways. In this manner, we will be strengthened to walk from the Valley of Despair and empowered to walk on the road which leads to the Mountaintop of Praise. Remember, God said, "Habakkuk, I am doing something in your days."[32] Friend, God is doing something in your day, in your life! Walk on!

---

[32]   Habakkuk 1:5

REFLECTIONS

1. Have you, like the student at seminary, found yourself facing an unexpected test in your life?

2. How did you respond to the test?

3. Have you found yourself putting on the false mask, "Oh, I'm fine," to hide your pain?

4. Have you found yourself wondering if God really was present in your life?

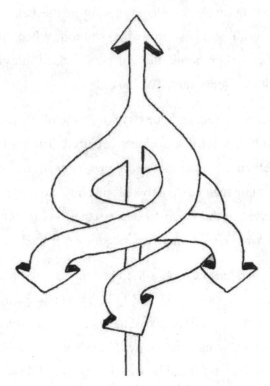

CHAPTER THREE
THREE ROCKY ROADS

Art Thou not from everlasting,
O LORD, my God, my Holy One?
Thine eyes are too pure to approve evil,
And Thou canst not look on wickedness with favor.
Why dost Thou look with favor
on those who deal treacherously?
Why are Thou silent when the wicked swallowed up
Those more righteous than they?

HABAKKUK 1:12–13

There is an old Chinese story about a father and his two sons. One day as the two sons were working in the fields, they captured a beautiful and powerful white stallion. When the two sons brought the stallion home, the villagers praised the young men. The old father simply said, "We'll see."

A few years passed, and one day while one of the sons was riding the stallion, a terrible accident occurred. The stallion lost its footing, fell, and pinned the young man beneath its body. Tragically, the young man was paralyzed and could no longer walk. The villagers went to the father to express their great sorrow for the paralyzed son. The old man responded, "We'll see."

Several years passed, and a terrible war occurred and soon engulfed the small village. All the village's young men were conscripted into the army. Because of his injury, the paralyzed son was exempt from enlisting in the army. The villagers went to the father and told him how fortunate he was that his son did not have to go off to war. The old man replied, "We'll see."[33]

There is a great grain of truth for us to glean from this story: *the circumstances of life are not always what they appear to be.* We live in a fast-paced world. Events swirl around us on a continuous and daily basis. Oftentimes it is difficult for us to take an impartial view of these events. Too frequently we make snap decisions without knowing all the facts of a situation. We rush to judgment.

The Wise Teacher of Proverbs advises, "Better a patient man than a warrior, a man who controls his temper than one who takes

---

[33]   There are various versions of this story. Author unknown.

a city … He who guards his mouth and his tongue keeps himself from calamity."[34] Like the Chinese father, we need to wait patiently before we pass final judgment. Things are not always what they appear to be!

In summer 2007, I experienced an injury to my left knee—a result of years of running—which required surgery. Numerous incidents occurred during and after the surgery and turned a relatively simple surgery into a life-threatening situation. Two additional surgeries were required, which extended a six-week recovery period into a five-month period of hospitalization and rehabilitation. I still deal with the consequences of that injury.

During the early days of this trauma, an event occurred which was so ridiculous and illogical it defied common sense. After two weeks of being bedridden, I was permitted to start walking within my hospital room to attend to personal needs. On the second day of this new-found freedom, I was preparing to take a shower, and I placed my crutches against the wall. As I stepped into the shower one of the crutches began to slip, and in slow motion, it fell on my left foot. A wing nut of the crutch cut through my hospital sock and sliced into the third toe. Blood immediately gushed out. After some time, the nurses finally stemmed the flow of blood, bathed the deep cut with iodine, and bandaged the toe.

As far as everyone was concerned, the incident was over. But it would take six weeks for the toe to heal and only after special treatment by a specialist. What struck me and all who heard of the incident was "Why did this happen?" On top of all the life-threat-

---

[34]   Proverbs 16:32; 21:23

ening circumstances which I was experiencing at the time, why did such a seemingly meaningless event as a cut toe occur? Remember, things are not always what they seem to be!

When God told Habakkuk that He was going to use the fierce Babylonians as His tool of judgment against Judah, Habakkuk did not understand. He cried out, "God, why do You look with favor on those who deal treacherously? Why are You silent while the wicked swallow those more righteous than they."[35] Numerous challenges caused Habakkuk to cry out to God. Under the reigns of Kings Saul, David, and Solomon (1060 to 960 BC), the unified and powerful nation of Israel had been a major player in the ancient Middle East for over a century.

But around 960 BC, jealousy and greed resulted in civil war, and the once unified nation split into two small kingdoms—the Northern Kingdom, known as Israel; and the Southern Kingdom, known as Judah. For two centuries, these two greatly weakened kingdoms existed in a vacuum as the powerful nations of Egypt, Assyria, and Babylon fought for superiority in the region. Then, in 722 BC, the Northern Kingdom of Israel was reduced to rubble by the conquering Assyrians. The Southern Kingdom of Judah struggled for another 130 years to maintain its freedom. But, in their own time, Judah fell to the now dominant Babylonian Empire.

From 641 BC until 609 BC, during thirty-two years of King Josiah's God-centered leadership, Judah prospered and remained a free nation. A spiritual reformation swept across Judah in 625 BC

---

[35]   Habakkuk 1:13

and lasted for sixteen years.[36]Josiah's reign could truly be called a golden era. But, remember, things are not always what they seem to be!

Around 620 BC political and military conflicts swirled across the sands of the Ancient Middle East. Mighty empires were at war. Unfortunately, King Josiah plunged into this cauldron of turmoil. Trying to prevent an Egyptian army led by Pharaoh Necho II from joining the Assyrians in a fight against the Babylonians, King Josiah was tragically killed at Megiddo in 609 BC. For five years the Egyptians controlled Judah and placed puppet rulers on Judah's throne.[37]

In 605 BC, the Babylonians, led by their great ruler King Nebuchadnezzar, defeated the combined Assyrian and Egyptian armies at the Battle of Carchemish. In a history-changing victory, the Babylonians swept across the countries of the Fertile Crescent, down the land bridge of Judah, and into Egypt. They destroyed nations as if they were mere sand castles on a beach and ruled the Ancient Middle East with an iron fist until 539 BC. The Babylonian exploits are recorded in several Biblical books and in the annals of ancient extra-biblical records.

During the last two decades of foreign domination (609 to 587 BC), four puppet kings ruled Judah. History reveals that under the dominion of the Egyptians and Babylonians, these four kings submitted to the evil practices of Judah's conquerors. "They did evil in the sight of the Lord."[38] Wicked religious practices were

---

[36] 2 Chronicles 34–35
[37] 2 Chronicles 35:20–36:4
[38] 2 Chronicles 36:5, 9, 12

instituted, and "all the leaders of the priests and the people became more and more unfaithful and followed the detestable practices of the pagan nations and defiled the Temple of the LORD ... they despised God's words and scoffed at His messengers, the prophets."[39] In 587 BC, after continuous rebellion by Zedekiah, the last king of Judah, the Babylonians destroyed Jerusalem. The Hebrew people were taken captive into exile to Babylon, where they lived for nearly seventy years until 539 BC.[40]

Habakkuk, one of the prophets sent by God as a messenger to the people of Judah, probably observed and experienced personally the violence and injustice recorded in the first verses of chapter 1 of the book of Habakkuk. Such persecution undoubtedly brought about the outcry to God from Habakkuk. He could not understand why God allowed this violence and injustice to occur. Remember, things are not always what they appear to be!

In our search for answers to the paradox of God's love and His allowing evil to exist, we find there are several different roads to travel. Although each road appears to be satisfactory, we will find that only one truly meets our needs as individuals.

The first road can best be termed as the "Rocky Road of Uncertainty." In the opening verses of his book, Habakkuk questioned— even challenged—God in an extremely blunt manner. Many in religious circles cringe at such actions and contend that Christians should never question, much less challenge, God. They believe such actions are akin to a lack of faith, perhaps heresy. However,

---

[39] 2 Chronicles 36:14, 16
[40] 2 Chronicles 36:17–21

as we share Habakkuk's encounter with God, we discover God is not threatened by questions; He is okay with our questions. In fact, questions reveal the true nature and depth of a person's faith in God.

As a member of the Temple choir, Habakkuk was familiar with the creeds and traditions of Judaism. He knew the heritage of the Hebrew people and the accounts of the many occasions when the Almighty God sheltered and delivered His people from terrible times. He sang psalms of praise like Psalm 121: "I will lift up my eyes to the mountains; from whence shall my help come? My help comes from the LORD, who made heaven and earth. He will not allow your foot to slip; He who keeps you will not slumber ... The LORD will protect you from all evil."[41]

He recalled the great promises of God like those recorded by the prophet Isaiah: "But now, thus says the LORD, your creator, O Jacob, and He who formed you, O Israel, 'Do not fear for I have redeemed you; I have called you by name; you are Mine! When you pass through the waters, I will be with you; and through the rivers, they will not overflow you. When you walk through the fire, you will not be scorched, nor will the flame burn you ... Do no fear, for I Am with you.'"[42]

Despite his religious heritage, Habakkuk walked on the Rocky Road of Uncertainty. He could not find comfort or answers to his questions in the creeds and traditions of his people. As far as the prophet could determine, God was silent, had hidden Him-

---

[41] Psalm 121: 1–3, 7a
[42] Isaiah 43:1–2, 5a

self, and could not be found: "How long, O LORD, will I call for help, and Thou wilt not hear."[43] Uncertainty and confusion confronted the prophet wherever he turned. God did not seem to care about His people!

In our world, those who hold a deistic worldview agree with Habakkuk. Deists believe God may exist, but He has distanced Himself from the affairs of this world and does not care what happens to us. Author James Sire comments on this deistic worldview: "In deism God is simply the abstract force that brought the world into existence and has largely left it to operate on its own. Deism holds that God makes no demand on His creation to be holy, righteous or even very good."[44] When asked about her spiritual views, one seventeen-year-old student remarked to the researchers of a nationwide study: "God's all around you, all the time ... [but] He doesn't talk back."[45] Habakkuk also felt this way!

At some unknown point in time, God responded to Habakkuk's pleas. God reassured the prophet He was not silent. He was at work in the world, and He did care about what was happening. God admonished the prophet, "Look among the nations! Observe! Be astonished! Wonder! Because I am doing something in your days. But you will not believe what you are told."[46] God was right! Habakkuk did not understand why a pure and holy God would use the wicked Babylonians to bring judgment upon the Hebrews, the chosen people of God.

---

[43] Habakkuk 1:2
[44] James W. Sire, *The Universe Next Door* (Downers Grove, Illinois: IVP Academic, 2009), 63
[45] Smith and Denton, p. 164; quoted in Sire, *Universe Next Door,* 63–64.
[46] Habakkuk 1:5

Why would God allow evil to reign over good?

Neither can we understand such actions. A popular book, written by author Rabbi Harold Kushner, is entitled *Why Do Bad Things Happen to Good People*? The book resonates with our mind and spirit because bad things do happen to good people. Like Habakkuk we are confronted with the paradox of a loving and just God who allows bad things to happen in the lives of people. The Rocky Road of Uncertainty is well traveled, but it does not lead us to a correct understanding of life.

A second road often traveled by people on the journey of life and faith is called the "Silent Road of Submission." This road is traveled by and recommended by many Christians. In his book *The Tracks of Fellow Struggler*, John Claypool relates that during the period he watched his daughter die from leukemia, many well-meaning Christians advised him to take this road. They came to him and said: "John, we must not question God. We must not try to understand. We have no right to ask or to inquire about God's will. He causes all things to work together for good to those who love Him."[47] It is hard to argue against these seemingly biblically based statements. They are so theological and churchy! Job's three friends used the same arguments. They repeatedly argued that Job had no right to question the actions of the Almighty God.[48]

We overlook the fact many biblical persons challenged God as they sought to understand His actions. Abraham and Sarah laughed when God told them He was going to give them a son. Ja-

---

[47] Claypool, *Fellow Struggler*, 72.
[48] Job 5, 8, 11, 15

cob wrestled all night with God as he sought to know God's will. Moses and the prophet Jeremiah challenged God's call to ministry. Hannah pleaded with God unceasingly for a long time until finally God gave her a son. Jesus Christ cried out to God the Father during His agony in the Garden and on the Cross: "My God, My God, why hast Thou forsaken Me?"[49] Yes, Habakkuk walked in an elite circle of biblical men and women who challenged God. He did not take the Silent Road of Submission.

Nor should we travel it, because this road reduces all life to a mechanical process. It makes both God and man into inanimate and impersonal forces. This deistic worldview is invalid. The lack of interaction between God and man results in "people becoming like cogs in a clock." [50]

God is a living personal being who desires to relate and interact with each and every person in the world. At creation God walked and talked with Adam and Eve.[51] The apostle John states that God will once again "dwell among His people at the end of time."[52] And the apostle Paul writes, "God, the Father of mercies and God of all comfort, comforts us in all our afflictions."[53] Similarly, the Gospel author Matthew notes that Jesus came to gather the people to Him "as a hen gathers her chicks under her wings."[54] From beginning to end, the Bible records God's operation in our universe, that He cares about us and desires to have a relationship with every individual.

---

[49]   Mark 15:34
[50]   Sire, *Universe Next Door,* 65.
[51]   Genesis 2–3
[52]   Revelation 21:3
[53]   2 Corinthians 1:4
[54]   Matthew 23:37

Shortly after I became a Christian, the topic of discussion in a Bible class was God's will. At one point during the discussion, someone suggested we should travel the Silent Road of Submission. In my newness as a Christian, I blurted out, "God did not make me a robot. He did not make me like a computer to follow some programmed printout. He made me a person, not a puppet on a string. He made me with a mind and a will to interact with Him."

That is exactly what Habakkuk did. He interacted with and questioned God. We can do the same thing: we can question God. It is a greater act of faith to question God than not to question Him. Two types of people do not question God: atheists, who do not believe God exists; and agnostics, who contend the existence of God cannot be proved by reason. Neither believe in a real and personal God; neither choose to relate or interact with Him.

In the movie *God's Not Dead*, an atheistic college philosophy professor challenges a Christian student to debate the infamous statement "God is dead." Three periods of class were devoted to the debate, and the other students in the class acted as a jury to decide the outcome. Throughout the debate sessions, the professor mocks and ridicules the student's arguments that God is not dead. On two occasions, the professor threatens the Christian student not to make himself "look bad before the other students."

At the end of the third debate session, the student asks the professor: "Do you hate God?" The professor refuses to respond, but the student asks him a second and a third time: "Do you hate God?" In a fit of anger, the professor screams, "Yes, I hate God.

I *hate* God!" The student quietly looks at him and asks, "How can you hate someone who does not exist?" Stunned, the professor stands open-mouthed, without an answer. One by one the jury of students stand and vote their unanimous answer: "God is not dead." Yes, God is alive! He wants to relate and interact with us. The Silent Road of Submission is not the road God desires us to travel on the journey of life.

There is a third road which I entitle the "Dead-end Road of Total Knowledge." Like the Rocky Road of Uncertainty and the Silent Road of Submission, this road is also highly recommended and traveled by many people. Some want total intellectual understanding of why something happens. Others want neat and tidy answers to everything before they believe in God. It is a path many Christians travel as they put God in a box and conclude He operates only in certain prescribed ways, predetermined rituals, traditions, and creeds.

In his book *Disappointment with God*, Philip Yancey discusses this third road. He relates the story of a young man named Richard who was a new Christian and a brilliant scholar. While in seminary, Richard wrote a manuscript on the book of Job which was published. Later he experienced several adverse circumstances in life: his parents divorced, a girlfriend rejected him, his professional career faltered, and he went through a period of severe physical illness. Like Habakkuk, Job, and the young seminary student, Richard entered his own Valley of Despair.

Richard once spent an entire night in intense prayer seeking answers to his "why" questions. He received no answers: God was si-lent. In his despair, Richard turned away from God. Later, he came to Yancey and with bitterness asked, "Why on earth doesn't God answer? If He would just speak aloud one time so everyone could hear, then I would believe. Probably the whole world would be-lieve. Why doesn't He answer?"[55] Like the Pharisees of Jesus' day who said, "Show us, then we will believe,"[56] many people today walk the Dead-end Road of Total Knowledge.

What Richard, the Pharisees, and many Christians do not un-derstand is that the Dead-end Road of Total Knowledge is a false road. It is not true to Scripture; it is not true to life; it is not even true to science, our modern-day god. Our world has placed its hope in scientific knowledge, but scientific knowledge is neither total nor absolute. Compare a textbook of science written in 1920 or 1950 with one written today. Many changes and revisions have been made. Why? Because scientific knowledge is based on ob-servable data which is always open to further observation. Total knowledge is both impossible and uncertain. What may appear to be true today may be changed tomorrow because of new data.

Contrast scientists' ever-changing theories with biblical writ-ers' proclamations: "Even from everlasting to everlasting, Thou art God . . .You remain the same, and your years will never end"; "I the LORD do not change"; and, "Jesus Christ is the same yes-terday and today and forever."[57] Contrary to those who travel the Dead-end Road of Total Knowledge, a person who seeks an an-

---

[55] Phillip Yancey, *Disappointment with God* (Grand Rapids, MI: Zondervan Publishing House, 1988), 27–34.

[56] John 6:30

[57] Psalm 90:2; 102:27; Malachi 3:6; Hebrews 13:8

swer from God "must believe that He is and that He is a rewarder of those who seek Him."[58] The ancient Hebrew writer of Genesis did not try to prove the existence of God; he merely accepted God's reality: "In the beginning God."[59]

God does not change like a science book. He is absolute and unchanging, and His Word stands forever. The prophet Isaiah wrote: "All flesh is grass and all its loveliness is like the flower of the field. The grass withers, the flower fades ... but the Word of God stands forever."[60] Ironically, the French writer Voltaire proclaimed that within one hundred years of his time, Christianity would be swept away from existence and pass into the obscurity of history. Yet fifty years after his death, the Geneva Bible Society used Voltaire's house and printing press to produce stacks of Bibles."[61] One thing is certain: the Rocky Road of Uncertainty, the Silent Road of Submission, and the Dead-end Road of Total Knowledge have no answers for the journey of life and faith. All of them lead a person nowhere.

Do not despair! Habakkuk discovered a fourth road to walk: it is the "Narrow Road of Steadfast Faith." As we continue our study of Habakkuk's journey, we will find that it is the only road which will lead a person out of the Valley of Despair.

Beware! It is a challenging and daunting walk!

---

[58] Hebrews 11:6
[59] Genesis 1:1
[60] Isaiah 40:7–9
[61] "The Bible: Can We Trust It?" www.raptureready.com/rr-bible.html.

REFLECTIONS

1. How would you apply the Chinese farmer's approach to life's circumstances, "We'll see," to similar circumstances in your life?

2. Which road of life—the Rocky Road of Uncertainty, the Silent Road of Submission, or the Dead-end Road of Total Knowledge—would you say you have walked on, or are currently walking on?

3. Have you found satisfaction on the road you are traveling?

In a sudden twist of events,
life intervenes,
and we find ourselves
traveling a path
we do not know,
we have not anticipated,
and we are unprepared for.

Chapter Four
Steady the Course

I will stand on my guard post
And station myself on the rampart;
And I will keep watch to see what He will speak to me,
And how I may reply when I am reproved.
Then the LORD answered me and said,
"The righteous will live by faith."

HABAKKUK 2:1–2, 4

In fall 1995, Judith and I took a much-needed vacation to Estes Park, located north of Denver, Colorado. The previous three years as pastor of a growing church in Central Illinois had been long and demanding. As Jesus said to his disciples after a lengthy tour of preaching, "Come away by yourselves to a lonely place and rest a while."[62] We felt the same need. A fellow pastor told me about a woman in Colorado who rented cabins in Estes Park to pastors who needed to get away. I called her, and God's timing was perfect. She had one vacant cabin for the next two weeks.

After a relaxing three-day drive, we arrived at the cabin late in the afternoon on the last day of September. The location was perfect. Situated atop a wood-covered hill, the cabin looked out over the surrounding forest and mountain range. The leaves had started to turn colors, and the brisk cool fall weather made the crackling fire in the beautiful stone fireplace a welcomed and cheery sight in the mornings and evenings. We spent the days reading, hiking, bike riding, and browsing through the small mountain villages in the area. What a refreshing time it was. We literally did nothing!

One day we planned a bike trip high up in the mountains. We packed a picnic lunch, loaded our bikes on the van, and headed out. About an hour into the trip, we stopped at a rest area. A small sparkling crystal blue lake spread around three sides of the rest area. Judith wanted to stretch our legs, so we embarked on a walk around the lake, which was about a half mile trek. For some unknown reason, I stuck a couple boxes of raisins, a couple of power bars, and a couple cans of juice in the pockets of my parka. As we

---

[62] Mark 6:30–31

walked and talked for an hour, we came to the back side of the lake. Judith noticed a signpost which pointed to other trails, and she wanted to continue walking on one of them. A signpost said the trail was only four miles long. Though not part of our planned events for the day, we were on vacation. So, off we went—*up* the trail. I let Judith lead the way and told her whenever she wanted to turn back, we would.

It was a good thing I stuck some snacks in my pocket, and we were wearing our parkas and gloves. Four miles and four hours later—and 8,000 feet higher—we reached the end of the trail—on top of Flattop Mountain (12,324 feet), one of the many mountains in the Rockies. What a beautiful sight! The sun was shining brightly, the snow glistened on the slopes, and the dark green trees spread out below us—we had climbed above the tree line. We could see the Rockies for miles in every direction. We used our cell phone to call Judith's mother and the church's chairman of deacons to tell them where we were. In many ways, it was the high point of our vacation. Little did we know that in a few days the Air Force would deploy me on a lengthy and demanding overseas assignment. How timely God's vacation was for us!

What enabled Judith and me to climb that mountain? Even today Judith will tell you she does not know how she did it. We did not know where the trail led. We were not really equipped to make that type of hike. Honestly, we would probably not have taken the trail if we had known where it led. Remember, *it was not in our plans for the day*!

Is that not exactly what we do each day of our lives? We wake up, dress, eat breakfast, and go out the door of our homes. We have our agenda in hand, and our schedule for the day is planned down to the last minute. We are in our comfort zone, and all is well!

But in a sudden twist of events, life intervenes, and we find ourselves traveling a path we do not know, we have not anticipated, and we are unprepared for. We find ourselves walking in the Valley of Despair!

It does not have to be this way. We do not have to walk the Rocky Road of Uncertainty, the Silent Road of Submission, nor the Dead-end Road of Total Knowledge. As Habakkuk discovered, there is a fourth road for us to travel. It is the "Narrow Road of Steadfast Faith."

In the New Testament book of Hebrews, we read, "without faith it is impossible to please God."[63] Commonly called "The Faith Hall of Fame," chapter 11 of Hebrews records the actions of many people of the Old Testament. One phrase—"by faith"—is repeated throughout the verses. By faith Abel, Enoch, Noah, Abraham, Sarah, Isaac, Jacob, Joseph, Moses, Rahab, Gideon, Barak, Samson, Jephthah, David, Samuel, the prophets, and others believed and obeyed God. They lived by faith. Regardless of obstacles or persecutions, they did not shrink back, and they received "approval through their faith."[64] They walked the Narrow Road of Steadfast Faith.

This is a valuable lesson for us to glean from Habakkuk's ex-

---

[63] Hebrews 11:6
[64] Hebrews 11:4–39

periences. Note God's words: "Habakkuk, record the vision and inscribe it on tablets that the one who reads it may run. For the vision is yet for the appointed time; it hastens toward the goal, and it will not fail. Though it tarries, wait for it; for it will certainly come, it will not delay. But, the righteous will live by faith."[65]

"To wait on God" does not mean to sit down and do nothing. In times of difficulties it is easy to withdraw from life and let the world pass by. That is not what Habakkuk did. He "stood on his guard post and stationed himself on the rampart and kept watch to see how God would answer him."[66] The prophet was like a soldier who walks his sentry post on the lookout for any enemy activity that threatens his city or army. Habakkuk understood that despite the circumstances which confronted him, life goes on.

John Claypool expressed a similar thought as he reflected on the death of his daughter from leukemia. In his book *Tracks of a Fellow Struggler,* he quoted Harry Emerson Fosdick, a famous American preacher of the early twentieth century: "A man can put off making up his mind, but he cannot put off making up his life."[67] Claypool then added, "We do not first get all the answers and then live in light of our understanding. We must plunge into life meeting what we must meet, experiencing what we must experience. And, in the light of living, try to understand. If insight comes at all it will not be before, but only through and after the experience."[68] Like Habakkuk, Fosdick, and Claypool, we must learn that life must go on even when we do not understand.

---

[65]   Habakkuk 2:2–4
[66]   Habakkuk 2:1
[67]   Claypool, *Fellow Struggler,* 28.
[68]   Ibid., 30.

One of the most challenging and desperate moments recorded in the Old Testament is found in the book of Ezekiel. The Hebrew people had been conquered by the Babylonians and deported as captives to the city of Babylon. Exiled from their homes and cut off from worship in their beloved and destroyed Temple, they cried out in despair: "By the rivers of Babylon we sat and wept when we remembered Zion. How can we sing the songs of the LORD while in a foreign land. . .? How shall we then live?"[69] God's answer was clear and simple: "live by faith."

Like the captives in Babylon and Habakkuk in Jerusalem, we must position ourselves to hear God. We must "stand on our watchtower" and listen for God's answer. We must not become too wrapped up in our problems—too caught up in the rat race of the world, too busy earning a living—to hear God! We are distracted by the concerns of life and cannot see God at work. Like the prophet, we need to take deliberate and specific action to spend time with God. We need to meditate on His Word, to be silent in prayer, to obey His commandments. Only then will we hear His still, small voice.

In the Hebrew language, the word for "faith" is translated "so be it." We use the Hebrew word all the time; it is the English word "Amen," sung at the end of many hymns and spoken at the end of every prayer. Do we really understand what it means? Whenever we use the word "Amen," we are saying to God, "So be it. Your will be done in my life. I will live by faith and trust You."

Remember the account about my cut toe in a previous chapter of this book? How the entire event seemed so meaningless? What an

---

[69]   Psalm 137:1, 4; Ezekiel 33:10

amazing lesson I was taught about faith through that cut toe. I came to understand what Habakkuk learned about waiting on the Lord.

After a two-week stay in the Army hospital where I had the knee surgery, I was transferred to Warm Springs, a civilian rehabilitation hospital. The evening I was admitted to Warm Springs, the resident doctor noticed my cut toe and asked me about it. When I told her the story, she was surprised that no further treatment had been done. She examined the cut and found it was infected. She had the nurses cleanse, treat, and re-bandage the toe. She also scheduled an appointment for me the next day at the hospital's Wound Care Clinic. After a lengthy examination, the Wound Care doctor immediately took aggressive action to treat the seriously infected wound. It took several weeks of continuous treatment for the toe to heal. That was only part of the story.

During the treatment of the toe, the Wound Care doctor observed that my lower left leg and foot were extremely swollen due to blood clots in my leg. The doctor had pioneered special treatment methods for this medical condition, and he implemented a three-week treatment program for my leg and foot. The treatment had a tremendously positive impact upon my ability to walk. At the end of the three weeks, a miracle happened: ninety percent of the swelling in the calf and foot had disappeared. The only swelling which remained was in the knee and thigh.

Think about it. If I had not cut my toe, I would not have seen the Wound Care doctor. He would not have treated the blood clots and swelling in my leg. Though I did not understand at the time why the toe was cut, God used it to bring a greater healing to my leg. He was doing something in my life, but I had to stand on my watchtower—more accurately, lie in my hospital bed—and travel the Narrow Road of Steadfast Faith to see what God was doing.

This path is the one all of us must travel. It was the road Habakkuk traveled as Judah was destroyed by the Babylonians. It was the road Jesus traveled on the way to Calvary.[70] It was the road the people of Hebrews 11 walked. When the trail becomes steep and narrow, walk on "by faith." As the apostle Paul stated, "I can do all things through Christ who strengthens me."[71] Remember, in the dark moments of life, God promises to never forsake you, and He will supply all your needs. You will reach the Mountaintop of Praise, just as Judith and I reached the highest peak of Flattop Mountain.

While he stood on the watchtower, Habakkuk realized another truth: *patience is essential to travel the Narrow Road of Steadfast Faith*. OK, forget this lesson! (*Just kidding.*) What American wants to learn "patience"? How true is the catchy phrase "Lord, teach me patience! Right now!" We live in a world of instant meals in thirty seconds, murder mysteries solved in sixty minutes, around the world news in eighty seconds, advertisements to lose ten pounds in five days, and the list goes on and on. If we cannot resolve an issue immediately, we cast it aside and move on to something else. Forget it if God does not answer our prayers by the end of our fifteen-minute "quiet time."

---

[70]　Luke 9:51
[71]　Philippians 4:13

Reflect a few minutes about the experiences of Habakkuk. How long did he cry out to God in chapter 1? How long did he stand on the watch tower in chapter 2? How much time passed before the vision of chapter 3 occurred? Our American sense of "instant time" distorts our understanding of the role time played in Habakkuk's life. Similar questions could be asked about the experiences of Job. Neither of their experiences occurred in a few minutes, hours, or even days. In both men's lives, the events occurred over a lengthy period of years.

From the text of chapter 1, we know Habakkuk started praying to God sometime around 625 BC. The references to the Chaldeans (Babylonians) point to their rise to power which extra-biblical historical sources affirm occurred in 625 BC. The vision of chapter 2 probably refers to God's judgment of the evil Judean kings who oppressed and treated their subjects unjustly during the period 609 BC to 587 BC. The text in chapter three indicates that Habakkuk lived to see all these events take place—a period of approximately thirty-eight years. The prophet had a long time to practice patience.

Another vital truth Habakkuk learned while standing watch on the tower was that *God is sovereign and in charge of all aspects of life*. The term "sovereign" is defined as "total and absolute control by a ruling king." For Habakkuk, the ruling king was "Yahweh," the God of Abraham, Isaac, and Jacob.[72] Yahweh brought the Hebrews out of slavery in Egypt into the Promised Land.[73] Yahweh chose the Babylonians to be His instrument of judgment

---

[72]   Exodus 3:6
[73]   Habakkuk 3:3–15

upon the evil kings and unrighteous people of Judah.[74] In time, Yahweh judged and destroyed the Babylonians for their wickedness.[75] By the end of his journey through the Valley of Despair to the Mountain of Hope, Habakkuk understood and acknowledged God's sovereignty. It enabled him to "live by faith." We, too, must learn this lesson!

Experiencing God's presence and control enabled Habakkuk to have patience, to persevere, and to endure the years of God's judgment upon Judah. As we will see in chapter 3 of his book, Habakkuk's belief in God's sovereignty gave him hope to walk through the "valley of the shadow of death" he witnessed and experienced in the last years of Judah.

We, too, must learn this lesson. Regardless of the circumstances in life, we must trust God's sovereign will to bring about His purposes. We can have hope in the darkest hours, peace in the worst storms, assurance during the longest nights, comfort in the loneliness times, and certainty in the most frightening turmoil.

How? Because God is personal and sovereign, He never leaves or forsakes us. He is in control and has a plan for our lives. "For I know the plans that I have for you," declares the LORD, "plans for peace and not wrath, to give you a future and a hope."[76]

In a discourse on the sovereignty of God, Oswald Chambers writes: "If God has made your cup sweet, drink it with grace. If He has made it bitter, drink it in communion with Him. If the

---

[74] Habakkuk 1:6–17
[75] Isaiah 36
[76] Jeremiah 29:11

providential order of God for you is a hard time of difficulty, go through with it. You must go through the crucible ... because in the crucible you learn to know God better."[77] All God asks is that we trust Him and have faith in His goodness. Habakkuk's constant faith in God enabled him to "wait until the vision came." As we travel the Narrow Road of Steadfast Faith, we must wait to see and hear God's answers!

In the opening verses of chapter 1 of his book, Habakkuk questioned God about another crucial issue: "The law is ignored and justice is never upheld. The wicked surround the righteous and justice comes out perverted."[78] In other words, if you are a just God, why is there injustice in the world? This question still baffles people today!

Justice is another element of the sovereignty of God. Who is in control: God or Satan? Good or Evil? In the latter verses of chapter 2, God reveals to Habakkuk that evil does not go unpunished. Without going into a lengthy commentary upon the biblical text, it is instructive to see how God exercises judgment upon evil.

Commenting on the evil actions of the Babylonians against the nation of Judah, God says, "All of them come for violence ... but they will be held guilty."[79] God then pronounces five "woes" upon the Babylonians. Woe is a Hebrew word which refers to "judgment." Each of the woes condemns the Babylonians—or any individual or nation—for their evil unjust acts.

---

[77] Oswald Chambers, *My Utmost for His Highest* (New York: Dodd, Mead & Company, 1935), 316.
[78] Habakkuk 1:4
[79] Habakkuk 1:9, 11

First, we read, "the soul is not right within the proud person."[80] Jeremiah, a contemporary of Habakkuk, prophesied a warning of God's coming judgment of Babylon. "This is what the LORD Almighty, the God of Israel says, 'I will punish the king of Babylon … I will bring a sword against the Chaldeans … and lay waste the land of Babylon … no man will live there.'"[81]

The Old Testament book of Daniel records God's punishment against Nebuchadnezzar, the great king of Babylon. One night as Nebuchadnezzar stood on the roof of his palace overlooking the magnificent city of Babylon, he remarked: "Is this not Babylon the great city which I myself have built as a royal residence by the might of my power and for the glory of my majesty?" While the words were still in the king's mouth, a voice came from heaven, saying, "King Nebuchadnezzar, to you it is declared: sovereignty has been removed from you and you will be driven away from mankind, and your dwelling place will be with the beasts of the field … until you recognize that the Most High God is ruler over the realm of mankind, and bestows it on whomever He wishes … and Nebuchadnezzar was deposed from his royal throne, and his glory was taken away from him."[82] All of Habakkuk's, Jeremiah's, and Daniel's prophecies came true. In August 539 BC., the Medes and Persians conquered the city of Babylon in one night.[83] Non-biblical historical records, such as *The Babylonian Chronicle,* affirm the conquest of Babylon by the Persians. Today, the ancient ruins of Babylon, located outside the present-day city of Baghdad,

---

80   Habakkuk 2:4
81   Jeremiah 50, 51
82   Daniel 5:30
83   Daniel 4:30–32; 5:20

still lie uninhabited. God's justice was fulfilled!

The issue of evil and justice is about God's sovereign will and authority. Rather than acknowledge the sovereign power of God, the Babylonians believed "their justice and authority originated within themselves ... their strength was their god."[84] The ancient Babylonians exemplified the present-day attitude: "It's all about me." From there it is a small step to commit evil and injustice against people less fortunate, poorer, and weaker. To God it does not matter if an individual is king of an ancient empire, CEO of an industrial conglomerate, president of a labor union, a murderer, or an abusive parent. Evil and injustice are a slap in the face of God. It will not go unpunished! As Habakkuk wrote: "The cup of wrath in the LORD'S right hand will come around to you, and utter disgrace will come upon your glory."[85]

One other action of evil—idolatry—is condemned by God at the close of chapter 2 of the book of Habakkuk. Unfortunately, when we of the twenty-first century read about idolatry in the Old Testament, we disregard the writers' words. Idolatry is outdated and not relevant in the present-day world. No one worships idols anymore. However, remember: all things are not always as they appear to be!

Our mistake is a lack of understanding what idolatry means. It does not simply mean to worship and bow down before some wooden or stone or gold or silver figure. Notice how Habakkuk describes the idols of his day: "speechless with no breath at all

---

[84]   Habakkuk 1:7, 11
[85]   Habakkuk 2:16

inside it."[86] The real meaning of an idol is anything which comes between God and *you*. We cannot deny that idols have not come between God and us. Present-day idols may be a job, a large bank account, a flashy car, a palatial house, a time-consuming hobby, or the latest technological device. But the greatest idol today is *self.*

Habakkuk describes the idol of self: "For the idol's maker trusts in his own handiwork."[87] Sound familiar? We boast of our ability to accomplish any task, overcome every obstacle, and conquer all challenges. The idol of self exemplifies the old American adage "I pulled myself up by my own bootstraps," or, as Frank Sinatra sang, "I Did It My Way." We are our own idol!

Centuries earlier when God brought the Hebrew people into the Promised Land, He warned them against such an idolatrous atti-tude. "For the LORD your God is bringing you into a good land … a land where you shall eat food without scarcity, in which you shall not lack anything … Beware lest you forget the LORD your God … lest, when you have eaten and are satisfied, and have built good houses and lived in them and when your herds and your flocks multiple, and your silver and gold multiply, and all that you have multiplies, then your heart becomes proud … and you say in your heart, 'My power and the strength of my hand made me this wealth.'"[88] Have we not forgotten how God brought the first immigrants to the shores of America four hundred years ago and blessed them—and us—in unfathomable ways? We have truly fallen to our faces and worshipped idols—ourselves!

---

[86]   Habakkuk 2:18
[87]   Habakkuk 2:18
[88]   Deuteronomy 8:7–17

In contrast to man's self-centered idolatry, Habakkuk reminds us of the sovereign will and power of God. There is a clear link between the first and last verses of chapter 2 of Habakkuk's book. In verse one, the prophet states: "I will stand on my guard post and station myself on the rampart; I will keep watch to see what God will speak to me."[89] After hearing God speak, the prophet concludes the chapter, "Let all the earth be silent before Him."[90] Habakkuk understood it is only when a man or woman is humble they become aware of who God is and how much they need God. Isaiah also proclaimed this truth: "Woe is me, for I am ruined! ... For my eyes have seen the King, the LORD of hosts."[91] God is sovereign, not man!

Earlier I related the events that surrounded the running injury, subsequent surgery, and rehabilitation I experienced in 2007. With all that happened, it would be dishonest to say I absolutely walked the Narrow Road of Steadfast Faith. There were many rollercoaster rides of faith and doubt during this time. Like Habakkuk, I lay in my hospital bed many long, lonely, dark evenings, and cried out to God: "Why?" and "How long?" and "Why won't You answer?" As the days grew into weeks and months, visitors frequently asked how I was doing. I simply replied: "I'm so tired of being sick!"

During this storm, one truth I never questioned was the sovereign will of God. I hung on to my belief that He was in control of everything that happened. This conviction enabled me to persevere to the end. Faith gave me hope even when I received no an-

---

89   Habakkuk 2:1
90   Habakkuk 2:20
91   Isaiah 6:5

swers to my questions. As the writer of the New Testament book of Hebrews proclaimed: "Now faith is the assurance of things hoped for, the conviction of things not seen."[92] Like an anchor which holds a ship steady during a storm, our belief in God's sovereign will and presence is the spiritual anchor that will hold a person steadfast in any storm of adversity. "Habakkuk, I am doing something in your days ... though the vision tarries, wait for it, for it will certainly come, it will not delay.[93] We need to submit our heart, mind, soul, and strength to the sovereign LORD! Regardless of the situation, we will be able to walk on the Narrow Road of Steadfast Faith from the Valley of Despair to the Mountaintop of Praise!

---

[92] Hebrews 11:1
[93] Habakkuk 1:5; 2:3

REFLECTIONS

1. The title of chapter 4 is "Steady the Course." It is a nautical term which conveys the idea that we should maintain a steady course in life regardless of the situations we find ourselves experiencing. Would you say you are maintaining a steady course in your life right now? If not, what do you believe you could do to steady the course?

2. What situations do you find most unsettling in your life?

3. Have you found yourself living life by the "I Did It My Way" approach? How would you like to change that way?

Overshadowing everything, an individual must endure the pain to finish the race.

CHAPTER FIVE
RUNNING THE RACE OF LIFE

Then the LORD answered me and said,
"Record the vision and inscribe it on tablets,
That the one who reads it may run.
For the vision is yet for the appointed time;
It hastens toward the goal, and it will not fail,
Though it tarries, wait for it;
For it will certainly come, it will not delay.
…But the righteous will live by his faith."

HABAKKUK 2:2–4

I enjoy running, and all my life I have been a runner. As a child, I grew up on a 500-acre farm in the hills of northeast Arkansas, and I ran everywhere. I was never on an official track team because the schools I attended as a child and teenager did not have track teams. However, my high school athletic coaches knew only one form of physical conditioning—and that was to run! In college, as a fourth-class cadet at the Air Force Academy, early ten-mile morning runs to Castle Rock or the North Gate were the norm. Plus, there were the "attitude correction" runs through Hell's Canyon, the Academy's obstacle course. Then, as an upperclassman, I was a cadre on the obstacle course training unit, so I was always running with the underclassmen. I was probably the only cadet at the Academy who enjoyed the obstacle course!

After college, I continued to run. The venues varied: park trails, forest paths, country roads, city streets, school tracks, or golf courses. Whether in America, Europe, or Vietnam, it didn't matter where I was: I ran. Not surprisingly, the movie *Chariots of Fire,* a cinema-biography of Eric Liddell, the "Flying Scotsman," is my all-time favorite movie. Like Liddell I feel the pleasure of God as I run. All of us can experience the same pleasure of God as we run the race of life and faith.

Several biblical writers—the psalmist, the Wise Teacher of Proverbs, the prophet Isaiah, and the apostle Paul—use the act of running to teach spiritual truths about life. As we think about what occurs when a person runs, we can readily see the parallels between running and life. A runner has a purpose, a goal to focus one's efforts. It demands training to run efficiently. Running is a "loner" sport, so the runner must look within his or her own spirit to overcome obstacles. If you run in an official-sanctioned race, rules must be followed to win the prize. Overshadowing every-thing, an individual must endure the pain to finish the race.

Each of these factors applies to a person as he or she runs the race of life and faith. The psalmist speaks of the inner spirit of the "champion rejoicing to run his course."[94] The Wise Teacher of Proverbs warns us to watch the path carefully so that "when we run we will not stumble."[95] The prophet Isaiah reminds us our source of strength is God, and if we wait upon Him, we will "run and not get tired."[96] The apostle Paul challenges us to "run in such a way that we may win and receive the victor's crown."[97] Approaching death, Paul looks back on his life and affirms that regardless of all the obstacles he faced, he ran the race, kept the rules, and endured to the end: "I have fought the good fight; I have finished the race; I have kept the faith."[98] We must have the same spirit to run the race of life.

As chapter 2 of the book of Habakkuk opens, the prophet is standing watch on his guard post. Greatly disturbed by the re-sponses of God to his earlier questions, Habakkuk prepares to keep watch until God speaks. He expects to be reproved—if God bothers to respond—and wonders how he will reply.[99] But then God answers, and I suspect Habakkuk was surprised by the an-swer. One thing is certain, God encourages and empowers Habak-

[94]   Psalm 19:5
[95]   Proverbs 4:12
[96]   Isaiah 40:31
[97]   1 Corinthians 9:24
[98]   2 Timothy 2:5; 2 Timothy 4:7
[99]   Habakkuk 2:1

kuk to continue his journey through The Valley of Despair to the Mountaintop of Praise.

In His response God tells Habakkuk to "record the vision and inscribe it on tablets that the one who reads it may run."[100] In this verse, God imparts several spiritual truths to the prophet. First, he is to *record the vision.* God's words are vital! We need to study His words as recorded in the Old and New Testaments of the Bible to know how to live life. Centuries before Habakkuk, God spoke to the children of Israel as they prepared to enter the Promised Land of Canaan. He said, "Keep the words of this covenant to do them that you may prosper in all that you do ... The Word is very near you, in your mouth and in your heart, that you may observe it. I have set before you today life and prosperity, death and adversity ... so choose life.[101] The Wise Teacher of the Book of Proverbs conveyed a similar truth: "Treasure My [God's] commandments within you. Keep My commandments and live ... Bind them on your fingers and write them on the tablet of your heart."[102]

A second truth God revealed to the prophet was *the people were to read the words and run.*"[103] The phrase "that the one who reads it may run" does not refer to the physical activity of running. It is a metaphor for the concept of living life. Some writers illustrate this phrase by the image of billboards posted along the highways of America. As people drive past the billboards, they can read the varied businesses' advertisements. In a similar way, the people of Judah will know how God wants them to live life.

---

[100] Habakkuk 2:2
[101] Deuteronomy 29:9; 30:14–15, 19
[102] Proverbs 7:2–3 [brackets mine]
[103] Habakkuk 2:2

A third truth that God conveyed to Habakkuk as he stood on the watchtower was that *"the race of life is to be run by faith."*[104] The Hebrew language is verb-based, and all Hebrew words are derived from the verb form of a word. The word "faith" is not a noun; it is predominately an action word, a verb. Faith is life in action, not just a belief or creed. Faith is revealed not by what a person believes, but by how he or she lives life. How a person "runs" is revealed not by if he or she reads God's Word, but if he or she incorporates the meaning of God's Word into their daily life actions. We can go to church every Sunday, but it is how we live Monday through Saturday which will validate whether we are "the righteous who live by his or her faith."[105]

God reveals a fourth truth to Habakkuk in these opening verses of chapter 2: *"The vision is yet for the appointed time; it hastens toward the goal, and it will not fail. Though it tarries, wait for it; for it will certainly come, it will not delay."*[106] Several significant aspects about "the appointed time" are important for us to understand. Many of them are contrary to the American way of life.

First, the time is *appointed,* but by whom? We want to control anything and everything which affects our lives. The single-most thing which we try to control is our time. The cliché is true: "Time is the most valuable thing we have." Witness the obsession with planning our time to the last second. Most people have some system of time management, and every hour of the day is filled with task after task and event after event. Soccer moms literally

---

[104] Habakkuk 2:4
[105] Ibid.
[106] Habakkuk 2:3 106

run from one event to another throughout the day as determined by their digital calendar. And, woe are they if they forget to post an event and miss it! Witness the new generation of electronics which enable people—all in a single gadget not much larger than a credit card—to have telephone, Internet, and multi-media access. We want to ensure that no matter where we are we can "appoint the time" for everything in our lives! Question: Who is controlling whom? The person or the iPhone?

Even churches have bought into the world's planning philosophy. Note the Five-Year Plans, Long-Range Planning Committees, Church Planning Calendars, and Strategic Planning Councils: all serve as churches' event managers. Read your Sunday morning church bulletin with all the upcoming list of church tasks and events, but make sure you have a digital calendar with you so that you can post the not-yet-filled-in-blanks on your weekly schedule. It will take longer to post the events than attending a Wednesday night prayer service. But who needs a prayer service; everything is already planned!

Biblical writers make it clear that it is God who "appoints the time," not man. Habakkuk writes: "Then the LORD answered me and said, 'Record the vision.'"[107] It was not the prophet's revelation, but God's. The prophet Isaiah records these words of God: "I am the LORD, that is My Name ... See, the former things have taken place, and new things I declare; before they spring into being, I announce them to you ... I make known the end from the

---

[107]   Habakkuk 2:2

beginning, from ancient times, what is still to come."[108] The Wise Teacher wrote, "There is an appointed time for everything; there is a time for every event under heaven."[109] We need to rethink our way of living life and acknowledge God's role in appointing our times. Only then will we be able to read the vision as we run the race of life and faith.

Another critical concept in God's answer to Habakkuk concerns the time when the vision will occur. Responding to the prophet's cry, "How long?" God did not give a definite time when the vision would occur; instead, the runner must wait for it to appear. Many people view the journey of life and faith as a 100-yard sprint which is over in ten seconds. However, the journey of life and faith is like a marathon race which takes several hours to run. The journey of life and faith is not over in a few seconds or minutes or hours or even days; it is a race which lasts a lifetime. This is a lesson which we need to learn, because it applies to many aspects of our daily lives.

First, *we must wait on God's vision*. We can understand the prophet's despair in chapter 1 as he did not see God at work to relieve the people of Judah from oppression and persecution. His repeated question "How long?" reflects Habakkuk's spirit of fear and uncertainty. In his time, there was a proverb which expressed the people's view of life: "The days are long and every vision fails."[110] But God replies, "Though the vision tarries, wait for it; it will not fail."[111] Unfortunately, this is not how we approach life.

---

[108]   Isaiah 42:8–9; 46:10
[109]   Ecclesiastes 3:1
[110]   Ezekiel 12:22
[111]   Habakkuk 2:3

We want to know every detail about what will happen before we will do anything. If we do not know, we simply stop what we are doing. I have some friends who literally plan every stop of a road trip down to the last minute. One time they had their trip all planned, the car loaded, and every detail completed before they went to bed. Imagine what happened the next morning when they woke up to find that the electrical power had failed during the night and their alarm clock had not gone off! God said, "Wait for the vision, it will not fail!"

After I returned from the Vietnam War in 1969, my family and I lived in England and Germany for five years. Some people do not like various aspects of living in Europe: the cultures are different, the languages are different, and even the sense of time is different. Perhaps it was this different sense of time that I enjoyed the most about living in Europe. The pace of life is much slower, and people do not live their lives by their watches or a day planner.

During our second year in Germany, Judith and I took a vacation to Austria for a week to ski. Some friends took care of our children so we could have time to ourselves. Somehow in the packing of clothes and completing all the details for the trip, I inadvertently left my watch at home. Now that would normally have been a major issue with me, because I have always been a time-conscious person. This trip was to be different.

We spent the entire week without ever being required to depend upon a watch. Breakfast—sweet rolls, hot chocolate, milk, or coffee—was whenever we woke up. After breakfast, we spent the mornings skiing on the beautiful Austrian mountain slopes until we were either tired or hungry. Since we were always with a group of other skiers, we all quit skiing at the same time for lunch—delicious hot, thick Austrian soups with breads, meats, and cheeses. A short nap was followed by more skiing in the afternoons until the sun went down. After a long hot shower and dressing for the evening, we enjoyed an abundant supper meal and mingled with the other skiers in various social activities. Few stayed up late in the evenings. Most of us were exhausted from skiing all day, so bedtime came early. We knew morning would come sooner than we wanted.

For an entire week, this was our daily pattern. We were cut off from all media, and time was not a factor in our lives; it was as if we lived in a different century. For certain, it was a restful week despite all the physical activity. I have always suspected that the week was restful because we were not driven by the pressures of time. Interestingly, one unusual thing happened when we returned home. For the next year, I did not wear a watch, because during that one week, I had learned how to live a different type of life: one not focused on time, but upon living each moment of each day to the fullest. Even now, I prefer to not wear a watch. How do you live life—focused on your watch and calendar, or upon the gift of life which God has given you? As the psalmist proclaimed, "This is the day the LORD has made; let us rejoice and be glad in it."[112]

One of the most common time-savers that people practice is stacking time. In other words, a person does multiple tasks at the

---

[112] Psalm 118:24

same time to cram more tasks into any given segment time of a day. It is very efficient, but could that be the reason that medical studies contend that many people suffer from chronic fatigue? One medical study revealed that Americans do not know how to use their leisure time to relax. We go on vacation but carry our tablet so we can check what is going on at our place of work. We go to a baseball game but constantly monitor our smart phone. Even movie theaters must remind us to turn off our cell phones so as not to disturb people watching the movie.

Second, God not only appoints the times, He also determines *the purpose for which the times are appointed*. This is another aspect of life which we seek to control in our self-centered world. We want to determine our own purpose in life, and it begins early in life. At about the age of two years, our children clearly expressed this characteristic. When confronted by a task, they would adamantly say: "I do it." They did not want any help from us; instead, they wanted to do it by themselves. Unfortunately, that cute saying as a child can evolve into a spirit of self-centered determination as the child matures. Instead of seeking God's purpose for their lives, most people set their goals based on the world's criteria. How do I get accepted to the *right* college? Am I in the *right* social or political or economic group? How do I climb the corporate ladder? Whom do I have to impress to get the corner office? How much money can I make if I move to another job? Few people seek God's leadership as they establish their goals in life. Their motto: "*I do it!*"

Listen to the words of God recorded by the prophet Jeremiah:

"For I [God] know the plans I have for you."[113] The writer of Proverbs said, "Man may plan his way, but it is the LORD who directs his steps."[114] We would do well to heed the advice of the ancient Hebrew father to his son: "Trust in the LORD with all your heart, and do not lean on your own understanding. In all your ways acknowledge Him, and He will make your paths straight."[115]

A third truth that Habakkuk teaches us about time is that *God's "train" is always on time*. When my family and I lived in England and Germany, we often traveled by train. We quickly learned that if the schedule said the train was to depart at 5:00 p.m., we made certain we were in our seats at 5:00 p.m. If we were one minute late, the train would be gone! The same punctuality applied to the arrival of a train; barring an accident the trains always arrived exactly on time. Hear what God said to the prophet, "Habakkuk, the vision … hastens toward the goal, and it will not fail. Though it tarries, wait for it. For it will certainly come, it will not delay."[116]

We are very impatient people. We find it difficult to take a long view of life; everything must be right *now*! Church committees want a new church program to bring instant success; young married couples want to have everything their parents have, but forget that it took their parents twenty or thirty years to reach such a standard of living; politicians want an instant and no casualty war, but do not want to pay the price for freedom; and the list goes on and on.

---

[113] Jeremiah 29:11 [brackets mine]
[114] Proverbs 16:9
[115] Proverbs 3:5–6
[116] Habakkuk 2:3

Henry Blackaby notes in his *Experiencing God Study* that God does not think or act in temporal terms; instead, He thinks and acts in eternal terms. It may take Him a lifetime to bring the vision to completion, to work out His purpose in a person's life. Remember that "the vision will not fail; wait on it." Sadly, we tend to not wait for Him to work out His vision on His timetable. If only Abraham and Sarah had waited on God to give them a son. Instead they took the vision into their own hands, and their impatience still has consequences in the Middle East!

We need to learn one last thing from the prophet's words about God's vision, *"It will not fail."*[117] It is interesting how we praise, even idolize athletes. Ted Williams compiled a lifetime batting average of .344 as an outfielder with the American League Boston Red Sox from 1939 to 1960. He was the last player to hit above .400 in Major League Baseball; he averaged .406 in 1941. This means that when Williams batted, he was successful only 4 out of 10 times; he failed 6 out of 10 times; yet he is considered the best hitter of all times. Michael Jordan was probably the greatest professional basketball player of all time, yet his field-goal shooting average was only .411. He, too, was successful only 4 out of 10 times, which means he failed 6 out of 10 times.

Understand that I am not degrading Ted Williams, Michael Jordan, or any other athlete. I am simply pointing out how God's values are different from our society's. We often fail in our actions and goals, but God never fails; He always completes what He sets out to accomplish. This is what God says about His Word: "So

---

[117]   Habakkuk 2:3

shall My Word that goes out from My mouth; it will not return to Me empty, but will accomplish what I desire and achieve the purpose for which I sent it." Again, God proclaims: "My purpose will be established, and I will accomplish all My good pleasure … Truly I have spoken; truly I will bring it to pass. I have planned it, surely I will do it."[118]

Referring to God's deliverance of the Israelites from the Assyrian attack on Jerusalem during the reign of King Hezekiah (713 BC), the prophet Isaiah witnessed how God accomplishes what He has purposed. Isaiah writes: "This is what the LORD, the God of Israel says, 'Have you not heard? Long ago I ordained it. In days of old I planned it; now I have brought it to pass.'"[119] Not only did God plan the Assyrian attack on Israel, He also planned Israel's deliverance; He accomplished everything He planned. God does not fail!

Writers of the New Testament refer numerous times to what God had spoken through the Old Testament prophets about the birth of Jesus Christ.[120] Jesus Himself affirmed that God always accomplishes what He purposes. In the Sermon on the Mount, Jesus said, "Do not think that I came to abolish the Law or the Prophets; I did not come to abolish, but to fulfill. For truly I say to you, until heaven and earth pass away, not the smallest letter or stroke shall pass away from the Law, until all is accomplished."[121] Each of us face times in our lives when it seems as if God does not answer our prayers, as if the words of God in the Bible are

---

[118] Isaiah 55:11; Isaiah 46:10–11
[119] Isaiah 37:26
[120] Matthew 2:15, 17; 3:3; 4:14; Mark 1:3; Luke 3:4; John 1:23
[121] Matthew 5:17–18

merely nice-sounding words, but never come true. Like the people of biblical times, we must learn and practice the lessons that they modeled for us. God always keeps His Word, His vision does not fail, and the righteous are to live by faith. Job perhaps said it most clearly: "Though He slay me, I will hope in Him."[122]

One is reminded of John Stephen Akhwari, the 1968 Olympic marathon runner from Tanzania. Early in the race, he was knocked down and badly injured. As the race came to its close, Akhwari was nowhere to be seen. Over an hour after all the other runners had finished, Akhwari entered the arena for the final lap. Spectators watched in stunned silence and amazement as he slowly limped around the track. Pain was evident upon his face and in his body. Some tried to assist him, but he refused all help. As he crossed the finish line and collapsed into the arms of his coach, one reporter asked, "Why did you do this? You are so badly injured. Why did you not quit?" Slowly, Akhwari lifted his head, and looking at the people, he said, "My country did not send me five thousand miles to start the race; they sent me to finish the race."[123]

God did not send us to quit the race of life but to finish it! As the writer of the book of Hebrews reminds us, "we must run with perseverance … and not grow weary and lose heart."[124] In this way, and in His time, God will accomplish His purpose in our lives as we run the race on the Narrow Road of Steadfast Faith. It is the way we will succeed and climb out of the Valley of Despair to the Mountaintop of Praise.

---

[122] Job 13:15
[123] "Top 10 Emotional Olympic Moments," (ListVerse, December 6, 2009), http://listverse.com/2009/12/06/top-10-emotional-olympic-moments.
[124] Hebrews 12:1, 3

REFLECTIONS

1. The psalmist speaks of the "champion rejoicing to run his course." Would you say that you are rejoicing as you run your course of life? If not, what is keeping you from rejoicing as you run life?

2. As you evaluate your life, could you say with the apostle Paul that you are running in such a way that you may win the race of life?" If not, what is hindering you from running to win?

3. Compare your attitude toward life to that of John Stephen Akhwari, the 1968 Olympic marathon runner from Tanzania, who did not quit the race when he was injured; instead, he finished the race.

4. Are there any obstacles in your life that are preventing you from walking on the Narrow Road of Steadfast Faith? If so, what are ways you can overcome the obstacles?

||||||||||||||||||||

Ultimately,
the great tragedy
of no vision
stifles all hope.

|||||||||||||||||||||||||||||

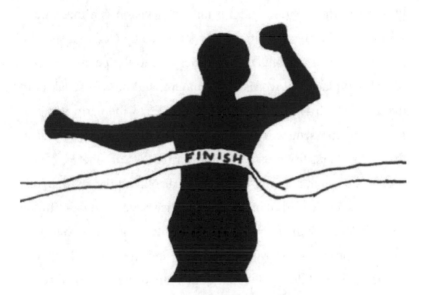

CHAPTER SIX
EYES ON THE FINISH LINE

Record the vision and inscribe it on tablets,
For the vision is yet for the appointed time
Though the vision tarries, wait for it,
For it will certainly come.

HABAKKUK 2:2, 3

The prophet Habakkuk is a fascinating writer who uses various forms of literature, different writing styles, and constant repetition of words and images to convey his ideas. For example, in chapter 2, verses two and three, he refers to a vision ten times. Obviously, this is an important idea for Habakkuk. Visions are mentioned throughout the Hebrew Old Testament. A vision is a message— sometimes visual, sometimes oral—revealed by God to a specific person who was to convey God's message to the people: "And I [God] will place My words in his mouth, and he will speak unto them all which I [God] command him."[125] In the early years of Israel, this messenger from God was known as a seer,"[126] but in the latter years, the most common term was "prophet."[127] Such prophets existed, not only in Israel but also in all the civilizations of the Ancient World; they could be either male or female. In the Hebrew Old Testament, we are most familiar with the two groups of men known as the Major Prophets and the Minor Prophets. These men lived during the kingdom years of Israel and were the writing prophets whose messages have been preserved in the canon of the Bible.

Other prophets—men and women—are mentioned in the Pentateuch, the Old Testament historical books, and in the New Testament. Abraham and Moses are called prophets, and there are other non-writing prophets, such as Gad, who guided David in his conflict with King Saul; and Nathan, who confronted King David about his adulterous sin with Bathsheba. There are also several

---

125   Deuteronomy 18:18
126   1 Samuel 9:9
127   Deuteronomy 18:15

references in the Old Testament to "schools" or "bands" of prophets. In the New Testament, John the Baptizer is called a prophet by Jesus, and Agabus is a prophet in the Early Church who prophesied of the imprisonment of Paul. Though he is not specifically called a prophet, clearly, John, the writer of the book of Revelation, with his vivid visions of the end times, performs the role of a prophet. Four women of the Bible—Miriam, Deborah, Huldah, and Noadia—are "prophetesses" in the Old Testament, and Anna and the daughters of Philip are prophetesses in the New Testament. Prophets were considered, along with the priests and kings, as the principle leaders in the nation of Israel.

The book of Habakkuk opens with the statement, "the burden (*chazon*) which Habakkuk, the prophet, saw."[128] Some scholars translate the word chazon as "oracle" or "vision." "The burden" is a specific message from God in response to the prophet's cry for understanding. As mentioned earlier the vision from God troubles Habakkuk, and he continued to cry out to God for understanding throughout the entire book.

Eventually God revealed His message to Habakkuk in what appears to be three separate visions: one in each of the three chapters of his book. In chapter 1, the vision is about God's activity in the world to bring judgment upon the sinful people of Israel. Chapter 2 is a vision of God's judgment of the decadent and oppressive people of Babylon. Finally, the prophet records his great theophany (vision) of the awesome and majestic God in chapter 3. Each of these three visions were intended for the people

---

[128] Habakkuk 1:1

of the prophet's time, but they also apply to us today.

What was God trying to teach the prophet—and us—through these three visions? I suggest that the message from God to Habakkuk revolves around the single great desire which all people have, particularly in times of distress—*hope*. As we study the book of Habakkuk, we see how the prophet moves from hopelessness to hopefulness on his journey of life and faith. Such a message of hope is of great importance for all people—then and now.

Though stated in negative terms, the Ancient Teacher's words, "without a vision, the people perish"[129] provides us insight into an understanding of the biblical concept of hope. Biblical translators have interpreted the Hebrew word for "perish" (*para*) in various ways. In the New American Standard Bible (NASB), the verse is translated "where there is no vision, the people are *unrestrained*" (emphasis mine); in the New International Version (NIV), "without a revelation, the people *cast off restraint*" (emphasis mine); in the English Standard Version (ESV), "without a vision, people are *discouraged*" (emphasis mine); and in the King James Version (KJV), "without a vision, the people *perish*" (emphasis mine). Without a vision, people experience discord, disturbance, despair, even death: an atmosphere in which there is a lack of hope. The possibility of no hope can prove devastating to a person.

First, "where there is no vision, the people are unrestrained" (NASB). Here the idea is that of a lack of discipline in a person's life. A vision serves as a guide to our actions; it provides direction. Imagine an army unit which has no orders. The soldiers do not

---

[129]   Proverbs 29:18

know *who* they are to attack. They do not know *when* to attack. They do not know *how* to attack. They have *no* objective. They do not operate as a disciplined army unit, but as a mob. There is no vision; therefore, they have no guidance.

In the Old Testament story when Moses goes up onto Mount Sinai to receive the Ten Commandments from God, para is used to describe the scene which Moses sees when he comes down from the mountain. The biblical text states: "Moses saw that the people were running wild and that Aaron had let them get out of control."[130] Remember Aaron had yielded to the people's desires and had made a golden calf idol for them to worship. How quickly the people had forgotten how Yahweh God had destroyed the idols of Egypt and brought them safely out of slavery. Without Moses' leadership ("vision"), the people were para. There was no vision, no guidance, no direction; the people were unrestrained and running wild!

For five years I taught high school sophomores at a Christian private school in San Antonio, Texas. In the fall semester, we studied Christian philosophy. During the course students learned the major worldviews which people have practiced throughout history.

One of the worldviews which was predominate during the late nineteenth and early twentieth centuries is known as nihilism, which means "nothingness." In the fullest and literal meaning of nihilism, nothing exists, even existence itself. While it was possible for me to draw graphics on a marker board to illustrate the other worldviews which humanity has practiced, it was impossi-

---

[130] Exodus 32:25

ble to draw nihilism. I simply pointed to the blank marker board and said to the students: "That is nihilism, nothingness. Even the marker board does not exist."

If you study the art of the nihilist period, you find that paintings, music, and plays reflect nothingness, meaninglessness, and chaos. For the artists, there is no vision. The ancient Hebrew writer of Genesis understood nihilism. "And the earth was formless and void, and darkness was over the surface of the deep."[131] It is the Hebrew writer's way of describing the chaos of nothingness.

Second, "without a vision, the people cast off restraint" (NIV). A primary belief of philosophical nihilists is that God does not exist. One of the main advocates of nihilism was the German philosopher Fredrick Nietzsche. His statement "God is dead" is a major argument of nihilism. However, what a person believes determines how he or she will act. Mitya, one of the Russian writer Dostoyevsky's characters in *The Brothers Karamazov*, states the nihilist's viewpoint with these words: "But," I asked, "how will man be after that? Without God and the future life? It means everything is now, one can do anything?"[132]

The Israelites exhibited this nihilist perspective at Mount Sinai. The people turned away from God and worshipped a golden calf idol, a non-god. They had "no vision and had *cast off restraint*" (NIV; emphasis mine). The people had rejected all authority and had chosen to do as they pleased. Watch today's news on the TV

---

[131] Genesis 1:2
[132] Fyodor Dostoyevsky, "A Hymn and a Secret," in *The Brothers Karamozov*, trans. Richard Pevear and Larissa Volokhosky. (New York: Farrar, Strauss and Giroux, 1990), 589.

or on the Internet. What do we find? There is moral chaos, and people do whatever they choose. There is no vision of God, and people have cast off all authority and moral restraints!

During the spring semester, I taught my sophomore students six major ethical decision-making systems which humanity practices.[133] The first approach is known as *antinomianism* from the two Latin words *anti* (against) and *nomos* (law). In its basic sense, this approach means people do not adhere to or obey any laws. They refuse to follow any guidance or direction; they do as they please. The Old Testament book of Judges is filled with violence, oppression, and injustice from the first to the last verse. In fact, the last verse of the book is a verbal description of antinomianism: "In those days, there was no king in Israel; everyone did what was right in their own eyes."[134] When there is no vision, people do whatever they want.

Try to imagine a world in which everyone does what he or she wants. This is exactly what the author William Golding envisioned in his book *Lord of the Flies*.[135] A group of young boys are marooned on an isolated and uninhabited island without any supervision. They have no rules, no guidelines, no vision, and like the people of Israel at Mount Sinai, they cast off restraint. In the end, Golding's "community" disintegrates into chaos and resorts to power to determine all actions. It is a nihilistic world inhabited by antinomian individuals. There is no community.

---

[133] Norman L. Geisler, *Christian Ethics*. (Grand Rapids, Michigan: 2nd Edition, 2010), 18–21.
[134] Judges 21:25
[135] William Golding. *Lord of the Flies*. (New York: Coward, McCann & Geoghegan, Inc., 1954).

Today's postmodern world reflects both nihilism and antinomianism. Morality in our society has slowly, but surely, eroded into *"whatever."* The phrase "if it feels good, do it" guides people's actions. Because of self-centerdness, immorality, and corruption, people have little confidence in their leaders. Justice goes to the highest bidder. Power is the law. How long can such a world of nothingness continue to function? Is it happenstance that the current popular genre of movies, such as *The Hunger Games, Divergent, Ender's Game,* and zombie or vampire films, portray dystopian worlds of nihilism and antinomianism? No vision—chaos!

Third, "without a vision, people are *discouraged*" (ESV; emphasis mine). Have you ever been part of an organization where there is no vision; where leadership has no vision? Within the organization, uncertainty is the reigning spirit; and, discouragement and despair fill employees' hearts and minds. Ultimately, the great tragedy of no vision stifles all hope.

In her novel *Atlas Shrugged,* author/philosopher Ayn Rand described a dystopian world which had descended into hopelessness. It all began when three adult children inherited a company which their father had built into a major enterprise. When they took leadership of the company, the three heirs lacked vision.

Their first act of leadership was to announce that from that day forward, every employee would be treated equally: every employee would receive equal pay regardless of position or responsibility—the lowest janitor and the top engineer; every employee would share their benefits with every other employee regardless

of their work ethic—the lazy slacker and the hard-working labor-
er; and, at the end of the year, every employee would receive the
same bonus regardless of gainful input or output—the moocher
and the producer.

Furthermore, leadership would be shared by all the employees—no more company boss, as their father had been, no more
managers or supervisors. Combined ideas from all employees
would be the way the new company-made decisions. The heirs
looked upon their new company as the first in a great social ex-
periment of collective equality which would lead the way into a
new future.

They had no vision, and there was no guidance. Everyone did
what they wanted. It was only a brief time before the employees
became discouraged. They had no hope! One by one, the leaders,
the thinkers, and the producers left the company. Within a year,
the company collapsed!

That was just the beginning. The visionless and hopeless mal-
aise spread across the country like a cancer until eventually "the
motor of the world stopped." One of the most frightening episodes
in *Atlas Shrugged* is a description of the "frozen" trains by Rand's
character Eddie Willers:

"We've had trains abandoned on the line, on some passing track,
in the middle of nowhere, usually at night—with the entire [train]
crew gone. They just leave the train and vanish. There's never any
warning given or any special reason, it's more like an epidemic, it

hits the men suddenly and they go. Nobody can explain it."[136]

Unfortunately, this same visionless and hopeless collectiv-
ist idea—the welfare state—is slowly spreading throughout the
world today. Many people have bought into the idea of entitle-
ment. They believe that simply because they live, they are entitled
to what others have earned through diligent study and hard work.
They have no vision for their lives. Like parasites, they mooch off
other people's visions. No wonder several generations of people
have followed in their parents' footsteps and now live in a state of
continuous welfare—living off the ideas and hard work of others.

Such is not a biblical teaching. The apostle Paul wrote: "Make
it your ambition to lead a quiet life ... to work with your hands ...
so that you will not be dependent on anybody."[137]

John Smith, the leader of the early American colony at James-
town, repeated Paul's words: "He who does not work, does not
eat."[138] One thing is certain: vision requires hard work. The re-
ward is a true hope for a better future.

This is Habakkuk's fourth lesson about vision: *a vision is necessary to guide a person through the challenges of life.* Have you
ever been around sheep? Without a shepherd to guide them, a
flock of sheep are helpless. When my children were in middle
and high school, we lived in a rural community in northern Texas.
Both children participated in 4H and Future Farmers of America
(FFA) and raised sheep for their school projects. Our home was

[136] Ayn Rand, *Atlas Shrugged* (New York: Random House, 1957), 630.
[137] 1 Thessalonians 4:11
[138] 2 Thessalonians 3:10

located about five miles outside the city and in the country. We had a large yard, and during the day, we allowed the sheep to graze in the yard. Because our house sat on the edge of a deep ravine, we tethered the sheep on long ropes. One day a ewe got loose from her tether and grazed right up to the edge of the ravine. Fortunately, the children saw her in time and caught her before she fell to her death.

Like the ewe who had no vision beyond the end of her nose, "people without a vision *perish*" (KJV, emphasis mine). Again, Ayn Rand's *Atlas Shrugged* provides us an insight into the meaning of a world without a vision. She writes: "Farmers were setting fire to their own farms, they were demolishing grain elevators … and, with no goal to reach save violence, they were dying in the streets of gutted towns and in the silent gullies of a roadless night."[139]

It is not just physical death which occurs without a vision; the scarier occurrence is the death of a person's soul. Many years later as he penned his Gospel, John reflected upon the events of the night of the last Passover Meal which Jesus ate with His disciples. John writes, "And after the morsel, Satan then entered into Judas … And, so after receiving the morsel he went out immediately; and it was night."[140] John was not merely commenting on the chronological time of day; he was referring to the nature of Judas' soul: "it was night." The darkness of the "night" led to its natural consequence: "Then, he went away and hanged himself."[141] Judas had lost his vision; he had lost his hope, and he perished!

---

[139] Rand, *Atlas Shrugged,* 943.
[140] John 13:27, 30
[141] Matthew 27:3–5

Stephen, the first martyr of the Early Church, experienced a totally different death. Even as the stones battered his body into oblivion, Stephen prayed, "Lord Jesus, receive my spirit. When he had said this, he fell asleep." [142] How encouraging to us as we experience the troubles of life—the stones thrown—and we walk like Stephen in Jesus' footsteps. With the vision of Jesus going before him, Stephen did not perish, he simply fell asleep, to awake in the presence of the sovereign God.

It is the same vision which Habakkuk had written on the tablets in chapter 2. He knew that at an appointed time, the vision would come and not fail. The vision of the majestic God in chapter 3 enabled the prophet to rejoice even during calamity. The vision was clear and certain. Habakkuk did not perish; he had hope; and, he walked with hind's feet on the heights of the Mountaintop of Praise.

In spring 2014, I traveled with my school's track team to the district, regional, and state track meets. During each of the meets, I observed a young female runner at three different races and was struck by her vision. At the starting line for the 100-yard sprint, while the other competing runners had their heads down looking at the track by their feet, she would take her position, lift her head up, and focus her eyes on the distant finish line. From start to end, she never dropped her head, and she never took her eyes off the finish line. This girl had a vision! And, she was rewarded! She was victorious in all three races and won the ultimate prize—first place champion in the state! She had her vision, she kept her eyes on that vision, and she gained the victory! I suspect she will live

---

[142]   Acts 7:55–60

her life the same way in the years ahead.

The apostle Paul reflected this same idea: "Do you not know that in a race all the runners run, but only one gets the prize? … Therefore, I do not run like a man running aimlessly [without a vision]."[143] What about you? Are you running like the young female athlete and Paul? Are you living, even in the face of death, like Stephen? Are you walking on the heights like Habakkuk? It is your choice! Remember: "Without a vision, the people perish."

---

[143] 1 Corinthians 9:24, 26 [brackets mine]

REFLECTIONS

1. In Habakkuk's times, God revealed Himself to the prophet through visions. How does God reveal Himself to us today?

2. Have you experienced a period of hopelessness in your life at some time? If so, how did you respond to the situation?

3. What vision do you use to guide you through your daily life?

4. Take a few minutes to write down at least three examples of chaos in our modern society.

5. What instances of night have you experienced in life? How did you find the light that helped you out of the night?

CHAPTER SEVEN
PEACE IN THE PRESENCE OF EVIL

For the earth will be filled
With the knowledge of
The glory of the LORD,
As the waters cover the sea.

HABAKKUK 2:14

Like other Old Testament prophets, Habakkuk's message is generally thought of in terms of prophecy which foretells the future. However, Habakkuk is different and is a unique prophet. In chapter 1, he is a philosopher. Habakkuk struggles with one of the most often discussed topics amongst philosophers—the matter of good and evil—an issue as relevant in today's world as it was in the prophet's times. How could an all-powerful, all-present, all-knowing God allow evil to exist and seemingly run rampant throughout the world? How could a just God allow such horrific events as the Inquisition or the Holocaust occur? How could a loving God stand by and allow a helpless child to be brutally abused by his parents or permit the innocence of a teenage girl to be viciously torn from her by gang rapists?

Such issues are not just the realm of philosophers; the common everyday person struggles with the same questions. When a precious five-year-old child dies of cancer, the parents ask "Why?" When a devout Christian wife discovers that her husband of fifteen years has been cheating on her with her closest friend, she asks "Why?" When a dedicated teacher and coach is terminated because he proclaims biblical truths in the classroom and attempts to instill principles of integrity in his players, he asks "Why?" When a trustworthy and hard-working employee is wrongfully accused of actions which he did not do and his "Christian" bosses allow the injustice to go unchallenged and fire him, he asks "Why?" Over and over, people cry out "Why," but evil continues with no end in sight. In Habakkuk's words, "How long, O Lord?"

Habakkuk is not only a philosopher, he is also an ethicist—a prophet who is deeply concerned about the day-to-day actions and lives of people. As a philosopher, Habakkuk understood that what a person believes determines his or her actions. As an ethicist, he also understood that what a person does reveals what he or she believes. In chapter 1, the prophet had questioned why a "good God" allowed evil to exist in the world. Over and over he cried out, but God did not answer. Perhaps the silence was part of what God was trying to teach the prophet about faith?

In His time, God answered Habakkuk's cries and assured the prophet that He was at work in the world and was in control of everything that occurred. God also told the prophet that eventually He would bring justice to an evil world. The climax of the message was God's challenging words: "The righteous will live by his faith."[144] During times of evil, every follower of God is to live by faith and know that God is always with him or her.

In His answer to Habakkuk, God refers to two groups of people: the righteous and the unrighteous. In God's mind, these are only two classifications in life: righteous and unrighteous; good and evil; narrow way and broad way; light and dark; day and night; life and death. This distinction is made countless times throughout all of Scripture. But society tries to create a third option: a so-called gray world in which there are no absolute laws, only relative ideas. A world in which a person can make his or her own laws and live as he or she chooses. However, such is not the case with God: there is no third middle-of-the-road way. There is either righteousness or wickedness, justice or judgment, and life or death!

---

[144] Habakkuk 2:4

Then, God proclaims to the prophet the judgment which He will bring upon those who practice evil in the world. In Hebrew literature, these verses are known as "taunt songs" and are a form of prophetic writings. A characteristic of taunt songs is the use of the Hebrew word translated "woe." This term is a word of judgment and points to the pending consequences of God's judgment upon evil. Five times the prophet uses "woe" in chapter 2. Each woe refers to specific evils which were characteristic traits and behaviors of the Babylonians. Their evil ways were known throughout the ancient world. Sadly, the same evils are prevalent in modern society.[145]

Verse 5 is a transitional passage between the prophet's vision[146] and the series of taunt songs.[147] The descriptive phrase "the haughty man" refers to the ancient Babylonians and the way they conquered the world of Habakkuk. After defeating the Assyrians and Egyptians in 605 BC at the Battle of Carchemish, the Babylonians swept across the countries of the Ancient Near East and "gathered to himself all nations and all peoples."[148]

Habakkuk's description of the Babylonians' brutal and cruel military tactics[149] is affirmed by secular historians. The *Nebuchadnezzar Chronicle,* housed in the British Museum, records the victories which made Babylon the ruling power of the Ancient Near East. Total war was their means to achieve world conquest. Their only desire was total power over everything and everyone.

---

[145] Habakkuk 2:2–19
[146] Habakkuk 2:2–4
[147] Habakkuk 2:5–19
[148] Habakkuk 2:5
[149] Habakkuk 1:6-10, 15-17

As Habakkuk points out, the Babylonians were "as greedy as the grave and like death never satisfied."[150]

History is filled with similar would-be world conquerors from ancient to modern times. In every case, a spirit of militarism goes far beyond mere military victories and seeks to re-mold every aspect of life of the entire society. The prophet Daniel records how Nebuchadnezzar attempted to change the culture of the Jewish captives taken in exile to Babylon: "he ordered that the sons of Israel be taught the literature and language of the Chaldeans."[151] A later attempt was made to destroy the Jewish faith by forcing them to either worship an idol made by Nebuchadnezzar or face death in a fiery furnace (a precursor of the Jewish Holocaust during WWII).[152]

Reflect on how militarism spread throughout the German society of the 1930s and 1940s. Nazism was not merely a political or a military movement. It was always the intent of Nazi militarism to first conquer the world and then change the entire world culture. It permeated the German church, the German arts, and the German educational system. It turned the German medical system into a human experimental system which brutalized helpless men and women. It started with the Nazi Youth and changed their minds to that of sadistic Schutzstaffel (SS) troops who created death camps to destroy millions of Jewish and non-Aryan people. If successful, Nazism would indeed have become a Thousand Year Reich!

Such a spirit of militarism still flourishes in the twenty-first

---

150 Habakkuk 2:5
151 Daniel 1:3–4
152 Daniel 3

century. Radical Islamic jihadists exhibit the same spirit. They indoctrinate the young. They feed on the emotions of the homeless and stateless peoples of the Middle East. They politicize and militarize a religion to gain the minds of millions of followers. Radical jihadists have one goal—to build a world caliphate, complete with a new mindset and new culture. As the ancient Hebrew Teacher wrote: "There is nothing new under the sun."[153] Militarism is alive and well in the world! We still, and will continue to, live in the presence of Evil.

The first taunt song pronounced by God against the Babylonians condemns covetousness: "Woe to him who increases what is not his."[154] Led first by Nabopolassar, and then his son Nebuchadnezzar, the Babylonian Empire's march across the Ancient Near East in the sixth and fifth centuries BC was unparalleled at the time. They conquered the Assyrians and swept across the Fertile Crescent, through Judah, and into Egypt, plundering, looting, killing, and destroying cities and fortresses. No one could stop them! They "were swifter than leopards and keener than wolves and fly like an eagle swooping down to devour ... they collect captives like sand ... and continually slay nations without sparing."[155] Every tyrant since then has followed the same pattern. Study the military actions of Genghis Khan, Napoleon, Hitler, and Stalin, just to name a few. They always wanted more of what was not theirs.

A second woe pronounced by God is against greed and injustice: "Woe to him who gets evil gain for his house, to put his nest on

---

[153] Ecclesiastes 1:9
[154] Habakkuk 2:6
[155] Habakkuk 1:8, 9, 17

high."[156] The prophet denounces the self-centered nature of the Babylonians who desired only to satisfy their greed. He uses metaphors of how even the stones and rafters cry out against the Babylonians' cruel injustice. It is one thing to obtain wealth through hard work; it is another thing to obtain it through violence, oppression, theft, and lies.

Unfortunately, nothing has changed over the centuries. Leaders from all areas of business, from CEOs to secretaries, embezzle funds that are not theirs. Trusted politicians and ministers break faith with the people they lead and do not do what is right, but what is best in their own self-interest. Constitutions of nations and covenants of faith have become meaningless words twisted to mean whatever the leader decides is best for himself or herself. Truly, it is a "shameful thing"[157] which is no longer an isolated scandal, but a common occurrence in our world.

God's third woe condemns pride exhibited through violence: "Woe to him who builds a city with bloodshed and founds a town with violence!"[158] As he walked on the roof of his royal palace in Babylon, King Nebuchadnezzar said, "Is this not Babylon the great, which I myself have built as a royal residence by the might of my power and for the glory of my majesty?"[159] What Nebuchadnezzar did not say speaks volumes about his character: pride, arrogance, self-centeredness, and cruelty. Babylon was built upon the battered bodies and shed blood of numberless captive Israelites and other peoples.

---

[156] Habakkuk 2:9–11
[157] Habakkuk 2:10
[158] Habakkuk 2:12
[159] Daniel 4:30

An earlier account in the Bible records how the Pharaohs of Egypt followed the same cruel policy: "So they appointed taskmasters over them [Hebrew slaves] to afflict them with hard labor. And they built for Pharaoh the storage cities of Pithom and Raamses."[160] A major target of ancient conquerors was captive peoples to be used as slaves who were a major economic resource.

Biblical scholars suggest that the reigns of the last four kings of Judah (609 to 587 BC) followed similar cruel practices and enslaved their own people. It is probable that God's woes in Habakkuk, chapter 2, were also directed against these evil kings.

Such slavery still exists in the modern world, ranging from economic slavery to human trafficking in women and children. Countless people are oppressed by political tyrants and militant jihadists. Regardless of the nation or the time, God clearly hates such oppression. In His time, "God will crush the oppressor."[161] Nebuchadnezzar discovered this truth when God drove him from his throne in Babylon and caused him to live as an animal for seven years.[162] Our world must recognize that the time will come "when the earth will be filled with the knowledge of the glory of the LORD."[163]

The fourth woe speaks volumes of God's judgment against man's unrighteousness, specifically drunkenness and immorality. Such evil actions affect not only the individual, but others. Habakkuk writes, "Woe to you who make your neighbor drink, who mix

---

160   Exodus 1:11 [brackets mine]
161   Psalm 72:4
162   Daniel 4:31–33
163   Habakkuk 2:14

in your venom even to make them drunk, to look on their naked-
ness."[164] The Babylonians were known for their drunken lifestyle;
even the Roman historians Herodotus and Xenephon write about
this character trait. The Bible also attests to their drunken lifestyle.
In Daniel 1, we read how King Nebuchadnezzar ordered a daily
ration of the king's choice food and wine to be given to the Jewish
captives. To his credit and faith, Daniel "made up his mind that he
would not defile himself with the king's choice food or with the
wine which he drank."[165]

Later we read of the drunken lifestyle of King Belshazzar "who
held a great feast for a thousand of his nobles, and he was drinking
wine in their presence."[166] He ordered that the holy vessels which
his father Nebuchadnezzar had brought to Babylon from the Temple of God in Jerusalem be brought to the feast so that he and his
guests could drink from them. The biblical account records that
the ungodly Belshazzar experienced the judgment of God as he
was slain by the Persian army which conquered and destroyed
Babylon that very night.[167] Truly, the Babylonians reaped what
they sowed.

We should heed the warnings of God about drunkenness. The
Wise Teacher warned, "Wine is a mocker and beer a brawler;
whoever is led astray by them is not wise."[168] The prophet Isaiah
also voiced a woe against drunkenness: "Woe to those who rise
early in the morning to run after their drinks, who stay up late at

---

164 Habakkuk 2:15–17
165 Daniel 1:8
166 Daniel 5:1
167 Daniel 5:30
168 Proverbs 20:1

night till they are inflamed with wine. They have harps and lyres at their banquets, tambourines and flutes and wine, but they have no regard for the deeds of the LORD, no respect for the work of His hands."[169] The results of drunkenness are unmistakable: "And these also stagger from wine and reel from beer ... All the tables are covered with vomit, and there is not a spot without filth."[170]

Yet "there is nothing new under the sun."[171] Our world has followed in the footsteps of the drunken lifestyle of the Babylonians. This woe of Habakkuk rings across the map of America, and the consequences are deadly. "In 2013, 59.4 percent of full-time college students ages 18–22 drank alcohol in the past month."[172] According to a 2015 National Survey on Drug Use and Health (NSDUH), "[Some] 86.4 percent of people ages 18 or older reported that they drank alcohol at some point in their lifetime; 70.1 percent reported that they drank in the past year; 56.0 percent reported that they drank in the past month. Excessive alcohol use led to approximately 88,000 deaths and 2.5 million years of potential life lost (YPLL) each year in the United States from 2006–2010, shortening the lives of those who died by an average of 30 years. This makes alcohol the fourth leading preventable cause of death in the United States. Alcohol problems cost the United States $249 billion on 2010."[173] A Centers for Disease Control and Prevention report states that "excessive drinking was responsible for 1 in 10

---

[169]   Isaiah 5:11–15
[170]   Isaiah 28:7–8
[171]   Ecclesiastes 1:9
[172]   College Drinking: Changing the Culture, "Statistics," www.collegedrinkingprevention.gov/statistics/prevalence.aspx.
[173]   National Institute on Alcohol Abuse and Alcohol, "Alcohol Facts and Statistics," www.niaaa.nih.gov/alcohol. Brackets mine.

deaths among working-age adults aged 20-64 years.[174]

These issues affect all Americans, whether they drink or not. A day rarely passes when an Internet story about drunkenness and the resultant sexual immorality is not recorded. Ninety-seven thousand students between the ages of eighteen and twenty-four are victims of alcohol-related sexual assault or date rape. Truly, as in the days of Habakkuk, drunkenness ravages the lives and homes in modern United States. Yet media continuously portrays that drinking alcohol is the fun and cool thing to do! Alcohol-themed commercials flood TV. Professional athletic teams are owned by alcohol corporations. Hollywood celebrities flaunt a drunken life-style. How blind we are!

We must not overlook the prophet's final words spoken against this woe of drunkenness: "The cup in the LORD's right hand will come around to you, and utter disgrace will cover your glory."[175] However, "the cup in the Lord's right hand" is not a cup of wine, but the cup of His wrath, of His judgment against the unrighteous of drunkenness.

Ironically, the apostle John refers to the Babylonians when he warns of the last days of humanity on earth: "And the great city was split into three parts, and the cities of the nations fell. And Babylon the great was remembered before God, to give her the cup of the wine of His fierce wrath."[176] Why do we continue on the path of drunken destruction?

---

[174] Centers for Disease Control and Prevention, "Fact Sheets–Alcohol Use and Your Health," www.cdc/gov/alcohol.
[175] Habakkuk 2:16
[176] Revelation 16:19

Interestingly, the fourth woe also deals with the violence the Babylonians dealt to creation itself. The prophet is perhaps the first Greenpeace environmental activist. Chapter 2, verse 17 refers to the wasteful ravaging of the land and animals of Lebanon by the Babylonians. As they swept across the nations of the Ancient Middle East, nothing remained in their destructive path. The prophet Jeremiah, a contemporary of Habakkuk, spoke of this ecological devastation by the Babylonians: "I looked, and behold, there was no man, and all the birds of the heavens had fled. I looked, and behold, the fruitful land was a wilderness, and all its cities were pulled down."[177] When the Jews returned to Israel after seventy years of captivity in Babylon, the land was desolate and the cities in ruins.

In the beginning, God granted dominion over creation to man.[178] He intended for man to act as a steward: one who takes care of the property of another. God did not intend for man to exploit and destroy creation for materialistic greed and self-glorification. Habakkuk's words were judgment against both the Babylonians and the evil Israelite kings of his time who enslaved their own people and exploited creation to build palaces, cities, temples, and fortresses for their self-glorification.[179]

In recent years, we have discovered—in some cases too late— how humanity's abuse of creation has wrought serious environmental consequences. These abuses have adversely affected our world and will continue to affect it for generations. Perhaps we

---

[177]   Jeremiah 4:25–26
[178]   Genesis 1:28–30
[179]   1 Chronicles 22; 2 Chronicles 2

Christians should become active members of Greenpeace. It is our Father's world!

The fifth, and final, woe proclaimed by Habakkuk is against idolatry, the worship of false gods: "Woe to him who says to a piece of wood, 'Awake!' to a dumb stone, 'Arise.'"[180] Scripture records the idolatrous worship practices of the Babylonians in numerous passages. Nebuchadnezzar took valuable articles of the House of the LORD God to Babylon and "put them in his temple at Babylon."[181] In the book of Daniel, we read that "Nebuchadnezzar the king made an image of gold … set it on the plain of Dura … and proclaimed that all peoples, nations and men of every language … were to fall down and worship the golden image."[182] Later we read of the idolatrous drunken feast given by King Belshazzar when "they brought the gold vessels that had been taken out of the Temple, the House of God which was in Jerusalem; and the king and his nobles, his wives, and his concubines drank from them. They drank the wine and praised the gods of gold and silver, of bronze, iron, wood, and stone.[183] Early in his book, Habakkuk describes the single-most important Babylonian idol, "they whose strength is their god."[184] How ironic that the modern world still worships that same idol—self!

Throughout the Bible, God warns His people not to worship the idols and false gods of the surrounding pagan nations. The first two of the Ten Commandments given by God to Moses warned

---

[180] Habakkuk 2:18–19
[181] 2 Chronicles 36:7
[182] Daniel 3:1–5
[183] Daniel 5:1–4
[184] Habakkuk 1:11

against idolatry: "You shall have no other gods before Me"[185] and "You shall not make for yourself an idol ... and you shall not worship them or serve them."[186] Throughout their history, the Israelites failed to obey God's warning.

All the prophets ridiculed the worship of idols and false gods. Why would one worship a "lifeless stone," a "block of wood which must be carried around," a "worthless figure in which there is no breath"?[187] Ezekiel compares the worship of idols with infidelity and prostitution.[188] Notice how Isaiah describes idols: "He makes a god and worships it; he makes it a graven image, and falls down before it. Half of it he burns in the fire; over this half he eats meat as he roasts a roast, and is satisfied. He also warms himself and says, 'Aha! I am warm, I have seen the fire.' But the rest of it he makes into a god, his graven image. He falls down before it and worships; he also prays to it and says, 'Deliver me, for thou art my god.'"[189]

The Hebrew writers used several words to refer to "idol." Used in combination with the Hebrew word for god (*el*), several of these words convey the meaning "nothing," "empty," "meaningless." Idols are literally "non-gods." God Himself affirms this truth: "I am the LORD, and there is no other; Besides Me there is no God . . .There is none except Me."[190] Yet humanity still worships idols. Are not media celebrities—whether seen on the screen or heard on a CD—simply new false gods raised up to be worshiped?

---

[185]   Exodus 20:3
[186]   Exodus 20:4–5
[187]   Habakkuk 2:19; Isaiah 45:20; Jeremiah 51:17–18
[188]   Ezekiel 16:15–43
[189]   Isaiah 44:9–17
[190]   Isaiah 45:5, 6, 18, 21, 22

Are not athletic stadiums, arenas, courts, and fields simply new temples for people to worship in? One will rarely find a church auditorium filled, but on Friday nights, Saturdays, and Sundays, countless athletic facilities will be standing room only. Like the ancient Israelites who "forsook the LORD and served Baal and the Astartes,"[191] we continue to walk in their idolatrous footsteps.

Habakkuk concludes chapter 2 with a triumphant proclamation: "But the LORD is in His holy temple. Let all the earth be silent before Him."[192] Such is the reality of history. Through the ages man has sought to lift himself up to the heavens, to revel in his own glory, to worship the works of his hands, and to proclaim himself as "God." He has failed time after time! History records the fall of one nation, one king, one dictator, one president after another. Man's fate is always the same. He returns to the dust from whence he came, and he takes nothing with him.

In time, Habakkuk's woes against Babylon were fulfilled. Secular and biblical history record that in one night the great city of Babylon was destroyed by the Persian army of Cyrus the Great in 539 BC. Since then the ancient city of Babylon has remained desolate. Despite the efforts of Iraq's now disposed dictator Saddam Hussein, "only 2 percent of the ancient ruins of Babylon have been excavated."[193] As prophesied by Isaiah, it is inhabited only by wild animals.[194]

How long before we realize the truth and heed the warning of

---

[191] Judges 2:10–13
[192] Habakkuk 2:20
[193] Arwa Damon, "Bringing Babylon Back from the Dead," CNN, April 4, 2013.
[194] Isaiah 13:19-22

Habakkuk and the other ancient Hebrew prophets. The shoe of the ancient Babylonians fits our world. The writer of the book of Hebrews warns: "It is appointed unto man once to die, and then the judgment."[195] Beware! "Woe! Woe! Woe! Woe! Woe!"

REFLECTIONS

1. Write down at least three events which seem to violate all sense of goodness.

2. Identify at least two ways that God can be seen at work in the world today?

3. Habakkuk writes of five evils which were practiced in his world. Give an example of each of these evils in today's world.

4. Hebrew writers use various words to refer to idols. The basic meaning of an idol is anything which comes between God and a person. Name at least three idols in our modern world.

---

[195] Hebrews 9:27

CHAPTER EIGHT
POWER IN PRAYER

A prayer of Habakkuk the prophet
according to Shigionoth:
"LORD, I have heard the report about Thee, and I fear.
O LORD, revive Thy work in the midst of the years,
In the midst of the years make it known;
In wrath remember mercy."

HABAKKUK 3:1–2

During the summer between my junior and senior years at the Air Force Academy, I spent four weeks touring military bases in the Pacific. At the end of the tour, I was assigned to Yokota Air Force Base in Japan for another six weeks. While at Yokota, I worked in the Wing Communications Division and was responsible for the security of daily communication codes used by air crews during their flight missions. Forty years later, I closed out my military career once again working in communications, this time at the Pentagon, as a member of the Joint Chiefs of Staff Communications Division, J6. It is interesting and inspiring how God oftentimes brings us full circle in our lives, and we can see how He has been working in our lives all those many years.

Such was the case with Habakkuk. Throughout chapters 1 and 2, Habakkuk confronts God with question after question as he seeks answers to why God is seemingly silent and absent from the world. In turn, God responds and challenges the prophet to *Selah* (Hebrew for "Stop, Look, and Listen") and to realize that He is active and in control of the world. As we turn to the pages of chapter 3, we find that Habakkuk has come full circle. Once again, he cries out to God, but now his cry is different. Earlier he was confused, angry, and bitter towards God; now he is humble, repentant, and trusting in the LORD. What brought about this 360-degree change in Habakkuk? What lessons had he learned?

Chapter 3 opens with a prayer by the prophet. Many excellent books have been written about prayer, and our walk with Christ is always strengthened as we deepen our prayer life. From Habakkuk's prayer, we learn several vital truths which will guide us on our journey from the Valley of Despair to the Mountaintop of Praise.

First, note how the text begins: "A prayer of Habakkuk the prophet, according to Shigionoth."[196] The Hebrew word *Shigionoth* refers to "a highly emotional poetic form." In other words, Habakkuk was filled with passion as he prayed; his prayer was "highly emotional." The early Puritans used to pray that they would be "filled with tears." Like Habakkuk, they were filled with passion and understood that prayer was a personal and passionate encounter with the Almighty God, not some intellectual or ritualistic duty.

What does prayer mean to you? One writer has said that prayer is the weakest element in people's lives and in church gatherings. Jesus frequently spoke about the necessity of "real" prayer. He considered the ritualistic, self-centered, and man-pleasing prayers of the self-righteous and hypocritical religious leaders of His day as meaningless babble.

In His teachings, Jesus spoke of prayer that brought a person into the presence of the Holy God. In one parable, a widow stubbornly refused to accept a judge's refusal to answer her plea for protection. She continually bothered him until in the end the judge listened to her plea and granted her request. She had passion.[197] Another account of passionate prayer is that of the publican who went into the Temple to pray. He was "unwilling to lift up his eyes to heaven, but was beating his breast, saying 'God, be merciful to me, the sinner!'" Jesus said that the publican went down to his

---

[196] Habakkuk 3:1
[197] Luke 18:1–8

house justified. He had passion.[198] Are our prayers passionate?

Throughout my life, I have listened to my children, grandchildren, and great-grandchildren pray at meals and at bedtimes. It is a joy to listen as they pray. Granted their prayers are not "churchy" and, sometimes, I cannot understand what they are saying, but their voices are always filled with excitement, with passion "according to Shigionoth." Do we pray with passion, or is it merely a ritual?

Second, we should pay attention to whom Habakkuk addressed his prayer: *"LORD."* As he has throughout his book, the prophet uses the ancient name of God—Yahweh (YHWH). This name of God is first found in Scripture when God revealed Himself to Moses at the burning bush.[199] When asked by Moses, "What is [Your] name so that I can tell the people in Egypt who sent me," God responded, "YHWH." God explained to Moses that "this is My name forever, and this is My memorial-name to all generations."[200] God further stated that this is the covenant name by which Abraham, Isaac, and Jacob knew Him.

It is significant that Habakkuk uses the name "YHWH" at the beginning of his prayer. YHWH is generally translated as "I AM." Some translators expand the meaning to "I Will Be What You Need Me To Be," which conveys the idea that God will always be there for His people and will meet their every need. Note that YHWH then says to Moses, "I AM indeed concerned about the people of Israel and what has been done to them in Egypt. So, I

---

[198]   Luke 18:9–14
[199]   Exodus 3
[200]   Exodus 3:13–17 [brackets mine]

will bring you up out of the affliction of Egypt."[201]

Remember earlier in chapter 1 of his book, the prophet had boldly challenged God's apparent lack of concern for His chosen people. He could not understand why God would allow His people to experience oppression and cruelty from both the evil Judean kings and the even crueler Babylonians. For Habakkuk, the "I AM" was MIA—missing in action.

In the latter part of chapter 1 and throughout chapter 2, God answered the prophet. God revealed that He is the Sovereign God, the I AM, who is in control of all that occurs in the world. He will bring judgment upon the unrighteous and wicked! The repetitive woes spoken by God[202] against those who are arrogant and wicked remind us of similar words by the psalmist: "Surely Thou dost set them in slippery places; Thou dost cast them down to destruction … O LORD, when aroused, Thou wilt despise their form."[203] God reaffirmed to Habakkuk that He is the same Covenant God, the same "I AM" who still cares for His chosen people.

As chapter 3 opens, Habakkuk again lifts his heart up in prayer. With great reverence the prophet acknowledges that YHWH is the God who delivered His people out of slavery in Egypt. The prophet understands that this same "I AM" will deliver His people once again. He is the Covenant God who will be faithful once again to His promises never to forsake His people. Since God is the same "yesterday, today, and tomorrow," we can have assurance and trust in YHWH as our Deliverer in times of trials and

201 Exodus 2:23-25; 3:16–17
202 Habakkuk 2:6–19
203 Psalm 73:18–20

sufferings. Evil will not conquer us! As the apostle Paul wrote, "If God is for us, who is against us … We are more than conquerors through Him who loved us."[204] Do our prayers acknowledge that God is the "I AM" in our lives?

Third, the focus of Habakkuk's prayer is particularly noteworthy: "LORD, I have heard Thy report" (Habakkuk 3:2a). The passage can also be translated, "LORD, I have heard the report about Thee." In both translations, the focus of the prayer is upon God, either about what God has done, or about God Himself. The same God-centered focus is further highlighted in verses 3 through 15 when the prophet has a third encounter with God.

What is the focus of our prayers? If we are honest, our prayers focus upon our needs, our wants, and our desires. Our prayers focus upon self, not God. We cry out, "God, where are you? Why do You not answer my prayers?" But there seems to be no answer! Why? Could it be that we, like the prophet, need to focus on God? Habakkuk heard and saw God because he was focused on God, not self!

Fourth, we need to understand the prophet's response when he heard the report about God; he said, "I fear."[205] Again, after his third encounter with God Habakkuk responds in a similar way: "I heard and my inward parts trembled; at the sound my lips quivered."[206] Like many biblical characters before and after him, the prophet expressed a "fear of God."

---

204 Romans 8:31; 37
205 Habakkuk 3:2a
206 Habakkuk 3:16

In the Garden of Eden, prior to their sin, Adam and Eve walked and talked with God. But, after their sin, they hid themselves from the presence of God. When God asked, "Where are you?" Adam responded, "I heard the sound of Thee in the garden, and I was afraid because I was naked; so I hid myself."[207] Another example of man's fear of God is that of Belshazzar, the last king of the Babylonians. Scripture records that "the king and his court were engaged in a great banquet drinking and praising the gods of gold and silver, of bronze, iron, wood and stone. Suddenly, the fingers of a hand appeared and wrote on the plaster of the wall. The king watched the hand as it wrote ... and his face turned pale and he was so frightened that his knees knocked together and his legs gave way."[208] This proud Babylonian king who was feared and dreaded by all the nations of the world and whose "strength was the Babylonian god"[209] fell in fear before the Most High God.

A great void exists in modern humanity's attitude toward God: there is no fear of God. Our world desires and seeks a softer and more comfortable image of God; we want a loving God. We do not understand a God who strikes dead a man who touches the Holy Ark of God to keep it from falling off a cart.[210] We cannot accept a God who causes Miriam to break out in leprosy simply because she speaks against the authority of Moses, her brother.[211] We turn away from a God who has a man stoned to death because he was gathering wood on the Sabbath.[212] We reject a God who

---

[207] Genesis 3:8–10
[208] Daniel 5:1–6
[209] Habakkuk 1:11
[210] 2 Samuel 6:6–7
[211] Numbers 12:1–12
[212] Numbers 15:32–36

strikes dead a husband and his wife who had kept back part of the money from land which they had sold, and then lied, saying they had given all of the money as a donation to the Church.[213] Yet "great fear seized all who heard what had happened to Ananias and Sapphira."[214] Why do we not fear God?

Our world has no place for such a God. Anyone who believes in the God of the Bible is intolerant, even a bigot. Modern humanity only wants a loving, compassionate, and tolerant God. He is merely the man upstairs. The apostle Paul spoke of such a time: "For the time will come when people will not put up with sound doctrine. Instead, to suit their own desires, they will gather around them a great number of teachers to say what their itching ears want to hear. They will turn their ears away from the truth and turn aside to myths."[215] Tragically, many so-called modern-day preachers of God's Word willingly accommodate their desires and tickle their itching ears.

The consequences for the Church and the world are deadly—read the list: school massacres—Columbine, Virginia Tech, and Sandy Hook; mass murderers—Charles Manson and Ted Bundy; financial corruption—Enron and Madoff; and sexual immorality—church leaders, government politicians, and athletic coaches. The list goes on and on. Every time one of these horrific events occurs, the world stands in shock and cries out "Why?" Media act like piranha in a feeding frenzy as they seek to outdo each other with the latest outpouring of rage against such acts. Many

---

[213] Acts 5:1–10
[214] Acts 5:5, 11
[215] 2 Timothy 4:3–4

pompous theories are thrown out by sociologists, psychiatrists, criminologists, and politicians, but no one has an answer!

The real reason for these terrible acts: *humanity no longer fears God*! Three millennia ago, the psalmist accurately stated this truth: "The fool says in his heart, 'There is no God;' they are corrupt, and their ways are vile; there is no one who does good."[216] Even as we face the reality of these tragedies, we deny the consequences of a world without God.

Personal choice is the new rule of law in the world; we do our own thing. Tolerance is the new watchword; everyone has the right to believe what they want to believe and to live whatever lifestyle they choose to live. The world has rejected all absolutes and has chosen a world of relativistic choices: a world in which each person makes up his or her own laws to live by and is his or her own god. Three thousand years ago, an unknown Hebrew writer evaluated his society and concluded his book with these words: "In those days there was no king in Israel; everyone did what was right in his own eyes."[217] No truer words characterize our modern world.

Beyond a shadow of a doubt, God has turned His back upon our world. Who can doubt that at some undetermined time in the future God will say as He did thousands of years ago, "I will blot out man whom I have created from the face of the land, from man to animals to creeping things and to birds of the sky; for I am sorry that I have made them … [because] every intent of the thoughts of

---

[216] Psalm 53:1
[217] Judges 21:25

man's heart is only evil continually."[218]

In the end, God will not bring a flood to destroy today's world of evil. This time He will bring fire to cleanse the world: "the heavens will pass away with a roar and the elements will be destroyed with intense heat, and the earth and its works will be burned up."[219] Eight hundred years earlier, the prophet Isaiah had spoken a similar warning: "For behold, the LORD will come in fire and His chariots like the whirlwind to render His anger with fury and His rebuke with flames of fire. For the LORD will execute judgment by fire and by His sword on all flesh, and those slain by the LORD will be many."[220]

Ironically, humanity will then fear the LORD. They will say to the mountains and to the rocks, "Fall on us and hide us from the face of Him who sits on the throne, and from the wrath of the Lamb."[221] But it will be too late! At that time God will not be a God of love and mercy. He will be the God of wrath and judgment!

The only answer for us is to turn to God in repentance, seek His face, and fear Him. The writers of Scripture continually admonish us to fear the LORD.[222] The philosopher of the book of Ecclesiastes concluded his search for truth with these words: "Now all has been heard; here is the conclusion of the matter. Fear God and keep His commandments for this is the whole duty of man."[223] Do we fear God? Like Moses at the burning bush, Isaiah in the Tem-

---

[218]   Genesis 6:5, 7 [brackets mine]
[219]   2 Peter 3:10
[220]   Isaiah 66:15–16
[221]   Revelation 6:16
[222]   Job 28:28; Psalm 34:9; 111:10; Proverbs 1:7; 3:7–8: 10:27
[223]   Ecclesiastes 12:13

ple, Daniel in the lion's den, and, Habakkuk in Jerusalem, we, too, must fear the LORD, the Almighty Sovereign "I AM."

In the last words of his prayer, Habakkuk makes three requests of God. What is noteworthy is that none of the three requests are for himself, something which is contrary to the prayers of many of us. Our typical prayer is focused on self, and the primary subject of prayer is things which will make our lives more comfortable. None of that is found in Habakkuk's prayer.

First, he prays: "O LORD, revive Thy work in the midst of the years."[224] With these words, Habakkuk acknowledges that the people of Israel have turned away from God in the years past. God is no longer their God, and they are no longer His people. A cursory reading of the history of Israel during the prophet's lifetime clearly reveals this fact.[225] The prophet's own words are evidence that the people had blatantly disregarded and violated God's commandments.[226] A spiritual revival was needed in the land.

Habakkuk also recognizes that spiritual revival is not something man can bring about by his efforts. Entertainment-style religious gatherings with big crowds, big budgets, big buildings, and flashy ear-tickling personalities will not bring spiritual revival. Instead, the prophet calls upon God to revive "Thy work." He remembers the words of the psalmist and acknowledges that only God can save the people: "O God, we have heard with our ears, our fathers have told us the work that Thou didst in their days, in the days of old ... For by their own sword they did not possess the land; and

---

[224] Habakkuk 3:2b
[225] 2 Kings 22–25; 2 Chronicles 34–36
[226] Habakkuk 1:2–4; 6–19

their own arm did not save them; But Thy right hand, and Thine arm, and the light of Thy presence, For Thou didst favor ... For I will not trust in my bow, nor will my sword save me. But Thou hast saved us from our adversaries.[227] In our trials, sufferings, and spiritual deadness, whom do we call—God or man? Habakkuk turned to God for salvation, not to man.

Second, Habakkuk requests, "in the midst of the years make it known."[228] The prophet uses the phrase "in the midst of the years" twice in two lines, clearly a significant concept he wants the reader to understand. Although he is fully aware of God's past great works, Habakkuk is not willing to live in the past glories of God. Nor is the prophet concerned about spectacular events sometime in the distant future. He is concerned with the needs of the moment.

Habakkuk cries out to God and pleads with Him to reveal Himself and bring His mighty arm to redeem His people—*now*—in his world. The prophet does not desire a supernatural miracle like the New Testament Pharisees who demanded Jesus to perform miracles so they could believe in Him.[229] This is not a lack of faith by the prophet; Habakkuk already believes in God and acknowledges His mighty work. It is not a "putting out the fleece" as Gideon did when he asked God to reveal Himself and affirm that He would be with the Israelites as they fought the Midianites.[230] Habakkuk knows that God is the Sovereign Deliverer of His people, and that on His timetable, God will once again deliver His people from the evil powers of the world.

---

227 Psalm 44:1, 3, 6, 7
228 Habakkuk 3:2c
229 Matthew 12:38
230 Judges 6:36–40

The key to understanding this phrase lies in the last word of the prophet's second request of God: "make it known." Too often when we think of God's work, we think only of His mighty deeds. While this is a possible understanding of this portion of Habakkuk's prayer, there is also another meaning. The Hebrew word translated by the English word "know" does not just mean "to have intellectual knowledge." In the Hebrew language, knowing is directly linked to a personal relationship between two people. It is the word used to convey an intimate marital relationship between a husband and wife.[231] "Knowing" is specifically used to refer to a "personal relationship with God."[232] Habakkuk recognizes that while the mighty works of God might bring temporary relief to the current situation, he realizes that it is necessary for the people to have a permanent relationship with God, if they are to be truly restored.

Perhaps he recalled the words of God to Hosea, an earlier Hebrew prophet. At one point the people who had turned away from God said: "Come, let us return to the LORD ... He has wounded us, but He will bandage us. He will revive us after two days; He will raise us up on the third day."[233] But God knew their repentance was mere words, bent only on temporary relief from their troubles. He replied to Hosea: "What shall I do with you, O Ephraim? What shall I do with you, O Judah? For your loyalty is like a morning cloud, and like the dew which goes away early."[234] Habakkuk does not want temporary relief for his people; he wants

---

[231] Genesis 4:1, 25
[232] 1 Samuel 3:7; Jeremiah 31:34; Hosea 6:3; John 10:14; 14:7; Hebrews 8:11
[233] Hosea 6:1, 2
[234] Hosea 6:4

them to have a permanent relationship with God. He wants the words of God fulfilled *now*: "And I will say to those who were not My people, 'You are My people!' and they will say, 'Thou art my God!'"[235]

This must be our desire today in our broken world! We must know and be known by God. We must enter an intimate and permanent relationship with the Sovereign Lord. Only then will His mighty works be known and acknowledged. Only then will our witness about God be meaningful.

The third and last request of Habakkuk in his prayer to God is both frightening and comforting. The prophet acknowledges the coming judgment of his people by God, and so he humbly petitions YHWH: "in wrath remember mercy."[236] Two aspects of the petition clearly stand out: "wrath" and "mercy." Like heads and tails of the same coin, these two attributes of God—wrath and mercy—coexist in God. They comprise the same coin—God's love. You cannot have one without the other.

Even as he grieved about the coming wrath of God's judgment, Habakkuk fervently prayed for God to show mercy to His people, "O LORD, in wrath remember mercy."[237] The prophet knew that YHWH was not just a God of wrath. Undoubtedly, he recalled the words of the psalmist, "Despite this they kept on sinning; in spite of His wonders, they did not believe … Their hearts were not loyal to Him; they were not faithful to His covenant. Yet He was merciful; He atoned for their iniquities and did not destroy them. Time after

---

[235]   Hosea 3:23
[236]   Habakkuk 3:2d
[237]   Ibid

time He restrained His anger and did not stir up His full wrath."[238]

In his anguish for his people, Habakkuk must have thought of the weeping prophet Jeremiah's comforting words to the people after the destruction of Jerusalem, "Yet this I call to mind and therefore I have hope. Because of the LORD's great love, we are not consumed, for His compassions [mercy] never fail. They are new every morning: great is [His] faithfulness."[239] He also remembered the words of Micah, an earlier prophet to Jerusalem, "Who is a God like you, who pardons sin and forgives the transgression of the remnant of His inheritance? You do not stay angry forever but delight to show mercy."[240] Habakkuk knew that the Old Testament God of wrath was also a God of compassion!

New Testament writers also proclaim God's mercifulness. The apostle Paul writes, "But when the kindness of God our Savior and His love for mankind appeared, He saved us, not on the basis of deeds which we have done in righteousness, but according to His mercy."[241] Over and over in the Gospels, we see the full expression of God's mercy in the life, actions, and words of Jesus Christ as He fed the hungry, freed those bound in chains, forgave the prostitutes and adulterers, restored sight to the blind and voices to the mute, empowered the lame to walk and healed the lepers, even giving life to the dead.

Yes, Habakkuk knew that the Father in heaven was merciful. His plea to the Sovereign God, is simple: "remember mercy."

---

[238] Psalm 78:32, 37–38
[239] Lamentations 3:21–23
[240] Micah 7:18
[241] Titus 3:4–5

Even so, our prayer for our world must be "remember mercy!"

I suspect that today many people are facing various types of difficulties. We often struggle during seemingly overwhelming challenges, some of which are a result of our own actions and words. We have a sense of failure and despair, but we do not know which way to turn or what to do. Truly, we feel as if we are walking in the Valley of Despair—confused, discouraged, and lonely.

Hear the words of Habakkuk and know the truth of his prayer in your life: "O Lord, revive Your work in my life, draw me once again into a close relationship with You, and have mercy upon me." Take a rest stop and experience the power of prayer." Call out to the "I AM," and you will receive God's merciful restorative healing and power. Once again you can sing a new song as you walk out of the Valley of Despair and reach the top of the Mountaintop of Praise.

REFLECTIONS

1. What is your view of prayer?

2. How would you describe your prayer life? Is it a ritual or a passion in your life?

3. What is the focus of your prayers?

4. Explain the meaning of the phrase "fear the Lord." How does it affect your life?

5. Has there been a time in your life when you have experienced an answer from God to a prayer in your life? Describe the experience.

Like mountain climbers, there are times when we need to retreat to a safe camp and refresh our souls.

CHAPTER NINE
MY DELIVERER IS COMING

God comes from Teman,
And the Holy One from Mount Paran.

HABAKKUK 3:3

As a child I read with excitement the published accounts of the efforts of mountaineers to climb Mount Everest and K2, the tallest and second tallest mountains in the world. Even now I have some Air Force friends who are engaged in climbing the highest mountain on each of the seven continents; they currently have climbed four of the seven. The stories of these mountain-climbing adventurers are awesome, exciting, and inspirational.

One of the most critical elements of climbing such mountains is to establish a base camp at the initial point of the climb. This base camp is the foundation for all the climbers' efforts to conquer a mountain. Subsequent safe camps are then established at various levels as the climb progresses up the mountainside. The purpose of these safe camps is simple: to provide a secure place for the climbers to rest after each segment of the climb as they prepare for the next portion of the climb. Even more critically, these safe camps are necessary for the climbers to retreat to in case of injury or bad weather. In 1953—the same year that Mount Everest was successfully climbed for the first time—an American team of climbers was unsuccessful in its attempt to climb K2. Because of severe weather and injury to one of the climbers, the team was forced to stay in their safe camp for ten days. Afterwards, they were unable to continue the climb and had to return to the base camp. There is a lesson in this for us.

Let's take a breather and reflect briefly on how far we have come on our journey of life and faith. Like mountain climbers, there are times when we need to retreat to a safe camp and refresh our souls.

At the start, we found Habakkuk mired in the Valley of Despair. Confusion, anguish, pain, even anger marked the prophet's life with great uncertainty. He could find no answers to his questions. The world, as he thought it should be, did not exist. Justice, righteousness, and security were nonexistent. Even his God was silent and absent. Habakkuk's theology was bankrupt; what he had been taught in the rabbis' schools did not appear to be valid. For certain, he could not understand the rampant chaos of his world which threatened to destroy all that was good. His "how longs" had been too long!

Even when He finally responded to Habakkuk's cries, God's answers made no sense to the prophet. Instead of turning away in despair, Habakkuk continued to press God to explain His actions. He "stood on his guard post, stationed himself on the ramparts, and kept watch to see what God would say."[242] He lived by faith and "waited for the vision which was for the appointed time, which hastened toward the goal and would not fail."[243] In the end, he walked through the valleys and on the mountains. We, too, if we will follow in Habakkuk's footsteps, will be empowered to complete the climb to the Mountaintop of Praise.

One of the most memorable events in my life occurred during a summer trip between my junior and senior years at the Air Force Academy. While stationed in Japan that summer, I spent a weekend on a climb up Mount Fuji, the most popular sightseeing site in Japan. After an all-night climb, I stood on top of Mount Fuji

---

[242]   Habakkuk 2:1
[243]   Habakkuk 2:3–4

(12,398 feet in height) just as the sun rose above the horizon. It is impossible to describe the awesome and spectacular sight which spread out before my eyes. In utter silence, I simply bathed in the beauty of God's world. Like Habakkuk, I entered God's holy temple of creation, and was silent before Him.[244]

After his prayer at the beginning of chapter 3, Habakkuk appears to take another path. The prophet is like climbers who when faced with a sheer face of rock they cannot ascend find another route up the mountain. Habakkuk's lengthy exposition about God, His magnificence, and His power seem to have no purpose, almost an unnecessary parenthesis in the book.[245] However, this revelation or theophany or vision of God is the key to understanding the prophet's conclusion and is a vital lesson for us. Without the vision, there is no meaning to the prophet's book. Habakkuk's vision is a "base camp"—the foundation of his faith—as well as a "safe camp" to retreat to in times of difficulties and challenges.

In a study of human society, we find that virtually all cultures have accounts of a longing for a deliverer—some person who will rise and come to their rescue from devastation and despair. Messiah-figures fill the pages of military history—Spartacus, Joan of Arc, William Wallace, King Arthur and others. Similarly, the list of fictional messiahs is countless—the Three Musketeers, the Lone Ranger, Zorro, Superman, Spider-Man, Captain America, and Wonder Woman. Biblical stories also recount the tales of numerous messiah-figures—Moses, Joshua, Gideon, and King David.

---

[244]   Habakkuk 2:20
[245]   Habakkuk 3:3–15

Biblical accounts differ from historical and fictional messiahs. Though many false messiahs proclaimed themselves as the promised Messiah, it was never a human person whom the Israelite people looked for as their messiah; it was always God who was their coming Messiah. He would be their Deliverer. It is this critical factor that the prophet recognizes as he faces the final ascent to the Mountaintop of Praise.

The Christian singer Rich Mullins has penned a powerful song of longing for the promised Messiah. In the song "My Deliverer,"[246] Mullins voices the very ideas of the prophet Habakkuk that God will keep His promise and send a deliverer to rescue the people of God. Throughout Scripture God promises His people that He will never forsake them. He will be their deliverer! Time and again God fulfills His promise and never breaks it. Habakkuk understands this promise of God and records it in chapter 3 to reassure us in our times of despair.

We must consider one other truth before we make the final assault to reach the Mountaintop of Praise. In recording his visions of God, Habakkuk uses a literary pattern which is significant. Three times he calls upon God in prayer, and each time God answers the Prophet, but in three different ways. That is a lesson for us to learn: *God never answers our prayers in the same way*. Unfortunately, when God responds to us in a way different from our predetermined ideas, we do not hear Him. We need to learn that we cannot put God into a box and assume that He will respond as we desire.

---

[246] Rich Mullins. "My Deliverer." Album. *The Jesus Record*. By Songwriters Chad Robert Cates, Tony W. Wood, Jason Walker. (Word Entertainment, July 21, 1998).

Habakkuk's first prayer in chapter 1[247] is literally a cry of anguish which erupted out of his belief that God was silent and not concerned about the evils of the world. In His time, God responded and reassured the prophet. He said, "Habakkuk, yes, I AM here. I AM aware of and care about the circumstances of your life. I AM in control of what is going on in the world."[248]

Reflecting upon this sovereign characteristic of God, Francis Schaeffer entitled one of his books *He Is Here*, and *He Is Not Silent*. That is a message which the prophet needed to hear and a message which we need to hear today. Regardless of the circumstances surrounding us, and during the hurts and sorrows which threaten to overwhelm us, we need to hear the comforting voice of God: "I AM here, and I am at work in your days." In a similar way, Jesus spoke of God's presence in our world: "My Father is always at His work to this very day, and I Myself am working."[249]

In his first prayer in chapter 1, Habakkuk had prayed to God for justice, and God had responded with a promise that justice would be forthcoming. Surely, God's response would satisfy the prophet, but, no, Habakkuk did not accept God's response. Now in the prophet's second prayer in Chapter 2, he again was filled with similar uncertainties and questions. The prophet cannot understand why God would use the evil nation of Babylon to bring judgment upon Israel: "Why do You look with favor on those [Babylonians] who deal treacherously?"[250] Even as he cried out in frustration as he pled for God's answer, Habakkuk chose a wait-

---

[247] Habakkuk 1:2
[248] Habakkuk 1:5
[249] John 5:19
[250] Habakkuk 1:13

and-see attitude. He said: "I will keep watch to see what He will speak to me."[251]

There is a valuable lesson for us to learn from God's answer. *We need to be careful what we pray for.* God may give us exactly what we ask for; but, we may find that His answer is not what we really want. Far too often, we have a predetermined list of options for God to follow. When He responds in a way different from what we expected, we are unsatisfied with His answer. Remember the prophet Jonah: he wanted God to pour out justice upon the city of Nineveh, the enemy of Israel; but, he was not willing for God to show mercy on the people of Nineveh.[252] Like Jonah: we want justice, but we are blinded to the mercy of God in the lives of other people!

Habakkuk then cries out to God a third time.[253] This time he does not cry out in self-centeredness. He does not ask something for himself; instead, he asks God to show mercy. This time God answers the prophet in a way only a few people in the Old Testament ever experienced. In response to the prophet's plea for mercy, God reveals Himself in all His majesty, glory and power.[254] God came to Habakkuk visibly, even as He came to Moses and Isaiah. At the burning bush and again on Mount Sinai, Moses exhibited humbleness, and God came to him. In the Temple, Isaiah exhibited repentance, and God came to him. Now Habakkuk voiced a heart of compassion, and God came to him.

---

[251] Habakkuk 2:1
[252] Jonah 3
[253] Habakkuk 3
[254] Habakkuk 3:2–15

Could it be that we rarely experience the presence of God because we do not exhibit God's nature in our lives? We cry out to God, but we cannot hear His still, small voice,[255] because we are too busy. We talk to God, but we do not have ears to hear what He says through His Holy Spirit.[256] We ask Him to provide our needs, but we do not seek first the Kingdom of God.[257]

We want to walk with God, but His presence is choked out by the cares of the world.[258] Could it be that if we lived out the gifts of the Spirit—"love, joy, peace, patience, kindness, goodness, faithfulness, gentleness, self-control"[259]—He would come to us even as He came to Habakkuk?

In chapter 3, God came to Habakkuk from two specific locations.[260] These locations are familiar places to the prophet and people of Israel. Teman and Mount Paran refer to the beginning and the end of the Israelites exodus from slavery in Egypt. The geographical references reminded Habakkuk that God is always faithful and in all circumstances. During the forty-year exodus through the wilderness, God provided the people's daily needs and protected them from numerous enemies. Once again, God reassures Habakkuk, "I AM here. I will take care of you in all that lies ahead of you."

When the sun is shining, the skies are clear, the roses are blooming, and, the birds are singing, it is easy for us to believe God is

---

[255] 1 Kings 19:12–13
[256] Matthew 11:15
[257] Matthew 6:33
[258] Matthew 13:22
[259] Galatians 5:22
[260] Habakkuk 3:3

faithful. When the sun is obscured by dark and stormy clouds, and the roses are wilted, we forget that God is faithful. Why? Nothing has changed!

As the Wise Teacher of the book of Ecclesiastes reminds us, "there is nothing new under the sun."[261] The mercy God showed the Israelites in the wilderness, the mercy He showed Habakkuk in Jerusalem, and the mercy He has promised us is the same. Even as God did not forget the Israelites nor Habakkuk, He will not forget us!

Once, during a dark and stormy time in my life, I came across a passage of Scripture which gave me a clear insight into the majesty, glory, and power of God. In a time of trouble as King Saul sought to kill him, David said: "The God of Israel spoke to me, 'He who rules over men righteously, who rules in the fear of God, is as the light of the morning when the sun rises, a morning without clouds, when the tender grass springs out of the earth, through sunshine after rain. Truly is not my house so with God? For He has made an everlasting covenant with me.'"[262]Those words spoken to my troubled heart reminded me that God was still present in the affairs of the world and in my life. Even when we do not see Him working, God is faithful!

The single word at the end of verse three—*Selah*—is another reminder for us to remember the faithfulness of God's nature. Habakkuk uses the word "Selah" three times in Chapter 3.[263] Used often by biblical writers, the word means "to pause; to re-

---

[261] Ecclesiastes 1:9
[262] 2 Samuel 23:3–5b
[263] Habakkuk 3:3, 9, 13

flect." It calls the reader to take time and reflect on the nature of God, His words, and His ways.

Selah calls us to meditate: an act encouraged by all the religions of the world. Meditation is almost a lost art in the rat race of the modern world. All of us have seen the large white "X" sign at railroad crossings which warns us to be cautious, to stop, look, and listen: a train might be coming. Few people, even Christians, take time to stop, look, and listen to the revelations of God. No wonder we miss His presence!

Another comforting thought is found in these words of the prophet about the coming of God. Note that God's coming is not merely a one-time event. In our limited view of time, we focus on the immediate event; we see only what is happening to us at that moment. Such is not the case with God. He sees all of eternity; time itself is eternal. Thus, He comes from Teman—the beginning—and from Mount Paran—the ending. As recorded several times in Scripture, God is the "Alpha and the Omega, the first and the last, the beginning and the end."[264] What comforting assurance for us to hang on to during the challenges of life! No matter what we face, God is there for us from the beginning to the end. He never abandons us!

In this third vision, Habakkuk meditates on the glory and power of God: "His glory covers the heavens, and the earth is full of His praise. His radiance is like the sunlight; He has rays flashing from His hand ... where His power is hidden."[265] Why have we forgot-

---

[264] Revelation 1:8, 17, 21:6, 22:13
[265] Habakkuk 3:3–4

ten this great truth? Our world glorifies the stars of Hollywood, the politicians of Washington DC, and the athletes of countless stadiums and arenas. Like the Babylonians of Habakkuk's time, the same desire for glory and power fills the heart of modern man. Glory and power are the golden plum. People will say and do anything to grasp it!

What is man's glory and power when compared to the glory and power of God? Habakkuk saw and heard the power of God, and he trembled. "He has rays flashing from His hand, there is the hiding of His power. Before Him goes pestilence, and plague comes after Him ... The perpetual mountains were shattered, and the ancient hills collapsed ... Thou didst cleave the earth with rivers, and the mountains saw Thee and quaked ... The sun and moon stood in their places." [266]

Centuries before Habakkuk's vision of God's glory and power, the patriarch Job wrote: "God stretches out the north over empty space and hangs the earth on nothing. He wraps up the waters in His clouds ... He has inscribed a circle on the surface of the waters at the boundary of light and darkness. The pillars of heaven tremble and are amazed at His rebuke. He quieted the sea with His power ... By His breath, the heavens are cleared ... but, His mighty thunder, who can understand?"[267] Later the prophet Isaiah captured this power of God with similar words: "All the nations are as nothing before YHWH; they are regarded by Him as less than nothing and meaningless ... He reduces rulers to

---

[266] Habakkuk 3:4–11
[267] Job 26:7–14

nothing."[268] Man is but a pigmy in the presence of El Shaddai, the Almighty God!

For Habakkuk, this vision of God's glory and power reassured him of God's sovereign presence. Faced with the coming destruction of his beloved city of Jerusalem and the death and captivity of his people, the prophet trembled and decay entered his bones. Even though everything he held dear in his heart would be devastated, Habakkuk continued to rejoice in the God of his salvation. He walked in total and undying faith because his deliverer was coming! *So is ours!*

REFLECTIONS

1. Share a time in your life when you longed for a deliverer.

2. What event brought about the need for a deliverer?

3. Describe the role meditation plays in your life.

---

[268] Isaiah 40:17, 23a

CHAPTER TEN
SAILING THE STORMY SEAS OF FAITH

I heard and my inward parts trembled;
At the sound my lips quivered.
Decay enters my bones,
And in my place I tremble.
Because I must wait quietly for the day of distress,
For the people to arise who will invade us.

HABAKKUK 3:16

The phone call came out of the blue. "Pastor, *please* come to St. Mary's Hospital. Our daughter is in labor and is having complications. We could lose both her and the twin babies she is carrying." Without hesitation, the pastor left a message for his wife and headed to the hospital. Little did he know what drama of life was going to play out over the next six days. Later he would give thanks to God for that fact.

It was a twenty-minute drive through the metropolitan city, but the traffic was light due to the lateness of the hour. As he drove, he wondered what had gone wrong. He had seen the young mother-to-be only two days earlier at her brother's wedding, and she had seemed to be doing well. Her countenance had shined with that special glow of pregnancy, and she had been a delight to all at the wedding.

He thought about how the spirited, vibrant child had grown into the young married woman and mother of a two-year-old son. Now she was about to give birth to twin girls. He remembered the joy of baptizing her as a preteen, and then walking with her—and her parents—through those challenging teenage years. She had always held a special spot in his heart, so joyous and fun-loving. He didn't know it, but that special spot was soon to be tested.

When he walked into the maternity ward on the fifth floor of the hospital, the young mother's parents met him. As they hugged him, he felt their tears on his face. He was instantly aware that the situation was very serious. "Pastor, there is only a slight chance that one of the twins is going to survive, and our daughter is also in danger." With those words, the stage was set for the next six days: days in which the reality of life and death would be played out in pendulous swings of the clock of time. Hopes and fears were intertwined in an unchanging cycle.

After spending several nights in the hospital room with the young mother and her family, plus lengthy visits each day, the final call had come on the sixth day: "Pastor, please come quickly! She is going to deliver in the next couple of hours."

Once again, the pastor made a speedy drive through the city to the hospital. Less than an hour after he arrived, the crisis came as she gave birth. This time there was to be no joy. The largest of the twins was stillborn, and the smallest was unable to survive and died within two hours. They were premature—only twenty-four weeks, but, oh so perfectly formed.

Everyone gathered around the hospital bed as the nurses placed the babies in their mother's arms. Tears flowed silently as everyone simply waited. Finally, after nearly an hour of holding her twin daughters, the young mother gave the babies to her husband. With head bowed and tears flowing down his face, the young father slowly took the babies to the hospital nursery where the babies would be prepared for their burial.

The family drew close around the bed for a final prayer, and two words into the prayer, the pastor knew this was going to be a time of great personal hurt, not just for the father and mother and family members but also for himself. Every word of the prayer was like a knife twisting in his heart. After the "Amen," he hugged the young parents and the other family members, and after saying his goodbyes, he turned and almost ran out of the hospital room. Deep sobs broke forth from within his innermost being. He had to be alone; he had to find some meaning to this seemingly meaningless tragedy. "Why, God? Why could you not let these babies live? *Why*???"

Habakkuk had reached a similar point in his journey. He had heard God's pronouncement of judgment upon the people of Israel. Although he did not understand why God would use the evil Babylonians to punish His own people, the prophet had come to acknowledge that God was in control of all events. He knew now that God was not silent and that He was doing something in the lives of the Israelites. Habakkuk was willing to accept God's sovereign right to use whatever means necessary to bring about His purposes in life. Even as he witnessed the spectacular vision (*theophany*) of God's "march through the earth,"[269] the prophet realized God was true to His unchanging character. He understood that God was present and sovereign—in all things!

During his fear and despair, we see the great faith which Habakkuk had in God. He proclaimed, "I must wait quietly for the day of distress, for the people to arise who will invade us."[270] The prophet did not run, nor did he hide; he waited quietly. Earlier he had said "I will keep watch to see what God will say to me."[271] Now that God had spoken, Habakkuk waited upon God to act; he knew the word of God was never void. He may have remembered the words

269 Habakkuk 3:12
270 Habakkuk 3:16
271 Habakkuk 2:1

of Isaiah who refers to the surety of God's word: "So is My word that goes out from My mouth; it will not return to Me empty, but will accomplish what I desire and achieve the purpose for which I sent it."[272] Here is a great lesson for us to learn from Habakkuk— *to wait upon the Lord God.*

We tend to do everything *but* wait upon God. Something happens, and regardless of the situation, we immediately plunge into action. Challenged by the unknown and filled with uncertainty and without any thought, we find the quickest and shortest answer to get us out of the present situation. We think only of the now, and we fail to understand that life is not temporal, but eternal. Remember, God had said to Habakkuk: "The vision is yet for the appointed time; it hastens toward the goal, and it will not fail. Though it tarries, wait for it, for it will certainly come, it will not delay."[273] In faith, the prophet waited.

Habakkuk did not just wait upon God; he waited quietly, which is something we do not do! When difficulties come into our lives, the last thing we do is to be quiet. The Ancient Teacher advised: "He who guards his lips guards his soul, but he who speaks rashly will come to ruin … and, he who guards his mouth and his tongue keeps himself from calamity."[274] Job had a similar spirit during his tragedies: "He did not sin in what he said"[275]; he waited quietly.

Reflect for a moment on the storm in Habakkuk's life. If historical dating is accurate, then Habakkuk experienced the death

---

[272] Isaiah 55:11
[273] Habakkuk 2:3
[274] Proverbs 13:3
[275] Job 2:10

throes and destruction of the nation of Judah, the city of Jerusalem, and the Holy Temple of God. Such experiences would have been a day of distress for him. The prophet's period of waiting quietly was a time of great sorrow, grief, and pain.

Jeremiah, a contemporary of Habakkuk, was known as the weeping prophet. He, too, witnessed the destruction of Judah and Jerusalem, and his laments are recorded in the Old Testament book of Lamentations. Six centuries later Jesus wept over Jerusalem as He saw the coming destruction of Jerusalem by the Romans.[276] Habakkuk, Jeremiah, and Jesus grieved over the sins of their people which brought God's righteous judgment. The young pastor had experienced similar emotions at the death of the premature infants!

How many people today are in distress over the spiritual condition of our country and world? How many of us "pray without ceasing"[277] about the unrighteous sins which mark our times?

Do we weep over Washington DC, Moscow, London, Paris, Berlin, Peking, Tokyo, Ontario, Mexico City, Tel Aviv, Riyadh, Cairo, Tehran, Canberra, and the other capital cities of the world? What would happen if Christians around the globe made a determined and passionate effort to "offer up entreaties and prayers, petitions and thanksgiving, for all men, kings, and all who are in authority?"[278] Would it make a difference?

Or are we concerned only about ourselves? Are we like King

---

[276] Luke 19:41
[277] 1 Thessalonians 5:17
[278] 1 Timothy 2:1-2

Hezekiah, who, when warned about the coming destruction of Jerusalem, simply thought, "There will be peace and truth in my days?"[279] The ancient Wise Teacher advised, "The prayer of the upright pleases God ... and, He hears the prayer of the righteous."[280] James, the brother of Jesus, penned similar words: "Confess your sins to each other and pray for each other so that you may be healed. The prayer of a righteous man is powerful and effective." [281] The Early Church "all joined together constantly in prayer,"[282] and "after they prayed, the place where they were meeting was shaken, and they were all filled with the Holy Spirit and spoke the word of God boldly ... and they turned the world upside down."[283] Habakkuk was a man of prayer; Jeremiah was a man of prayer; Jesus was a man of prayer; the Early Church was a people of prayer. Should we be any less?

"Waiting quietly for the day of distress" is the supreme expression of faith in God. In recent years, I had the joy of knowing and working with a young colleague as we taught in a private Christian high school. I watched as she struggled with the challenges of teaching (her first position), even as she walked with her husband through the trials of an incurable disease. She had decorated the walls of her classroom with numerous plaques and posters of varying shapes, sizes, and colors. All the plaques and posters had the same verse: "Be still and know that I AM God."[284] It was her way of remembering that God would sustain and deliver her

---

279 Isaiah 39:8
280 Proverbs 15:8, 29
281 James 5:16
282 Acts 1:14
283 Acts 4:31; 17:6
284 Psalm 46:10

through all the challenges and storms of life.

One day she told me about three separate incidents which had happened to her that day; all three had revolved around waiting quietly upon God. There was nothing she could do to resolve the incidents; she simply had to walk in faith that God would resolve the situations. And, He did!

At the end of the school year, she resigned her teaching position to remain at home and care for her husband as they awaited the birth of their first child. She knew God would take her through whatever storms she faced in the days ahead. As a going-away gift, I gave her another plaque with the verse, "Be still and know that I AM God."[285] It was my way of affirming her faith in God.

In the classic devotional book *My Utmost for His Highest,* Oswald Chambers writes,

> "God brings us into circumstances to educate our faith … Faith by its very nature must be tried, and the real trial of faith … is that God's character has to be cleared in our own minds. Faith in the Bible is faith in God against everything that contradicts Him—I will remain true to God's character whatever He may do."[286]

One final thought. If we are going to complete our journey from the Valley of Despair to the Mountaintop of Praise, we must be people of faith. To walk on during the storms of life, we must wait quietly on God in all circumstances. Will you commit yourself to that walk?

---

[285] Psalm 46:10
[286] Chambers, *My Utmost,* 304–305.

REFLECTIONS

1. Have you experienced a difficult time in your life when you had to wait quietly without knowing what the outcome might be? Describe the time and how you responded.

2. Describe something in your life about which you pray without ceasing.

Those who wait on the Lord will gain new strength.

CHAPTER ELEVEN
REACHING THE MOUNTAINTOP OF PRAISE

Though the fig tree should not blossom,
And there be no fruit on the vines,
Though the yield of the olive should fail,
And the fields produce no food,
Though the flock should be cut off from the fold,
And there be no cattle in the stalls...

HABAKKUK 3:17

We have reached the final leg of our journey. We have trudged through the Valley of Despair, and we have Sailed the Stormy Seas of Faith. Now we start the final climb to the Mountaintop of Praise. As we have traveled the Narrow Road of Steadfast Faith, we have learned several lessons along the way; lessons such as life is not a rose garden without thorns; God is not silent, He is at work in our lives and our world; God is not threatened by our doubts and questions; and He desires that we relate and interact with Him. But the journey is not yet over; there are still a few lessons to learn.

The prophet Isaiah provides vital instructions to those who would climb the mountains of life: "God gives strength to the weary, and to him who lacks might, He gives power. Though youths grow weary and tired, and vigorous young men stumble badly, yet those who wait for the LORD will gain new strength; they will mount up with wings like eagles; they will run and not get tired; they will walk and not become weary."[287] Habakkuk followed these instructions.

The first instruction is that those who wait on the Lord will gain new strength. Habakkuk understood what it meant to wait on the Lord. As the book of Habakkuk opened, the prophet had waited a long time for God to answer his many questions. When God finally did answer his questions, Habakkuk did not understand the answers. Trusting in God, the prophet went to his watchtower and waited some more until God provided a more comprehensive answer. Even that was not enough for the prophet. In the last chapter

---

[287] Isaiah 40:29–31

of his book, Habakkuk concluded that once again he must continue to wait quietly until the Lord fulfilled His work in the world.

Habakkuk was willing to wait, because he knew that "the righteous live by faith."[288] He understood that to wait on the Lord was an attitude of trust in God. As Isaiah said, "Those who wait for the Lord will gain new strength."[289] Whose strength? Yours? Mine? No; the strength we gain is God's strength, not ours. As the apostle Paul wrote: "Your faith should not rest on the wisdom of men but on the power of God … We have this treasure in earthen vessels that the surpassing greatness may be of God and not from ourselves. We are afflicted in every way but not crushed; perplexed but not despairing; persecuted but not forsaken; struck down, but not destroyed."[290]

Our problem is that we try to climb the mountains of life in our own strength, rather than with God's strength. I learned this truth from my children when they were mere infants. Almost the first words they spoke were "I do it. I do it." I am sure all parents remember the challenges they faced as their infants grew into children and then into teenagers and young adults: their constant desire was to be their own person. As they grew older, their words were more sophisticated, but the same message: "I do it. I do it." Even the American primary character trait—independence—is expressed in the mantra "the self-made person." To depend upon anyone else is a sign of weakness that we will not allow in our lives.

---

[288] Habakkuk 2:4
[289] Isaiah 40:31
[290] 1 Corinthians 2:5; 2 Corinthians 4:7

During the first summer I was a cadet at the Air Force Academy, we spent a week of Survival School in the Rocky Mountains. At the end of the week, we had to find our way out of the mountains back to the Academy. One particularly steep part of the mountains was known as Missouri Gulch. The name had been the idea of someone who used the motto of the State of Missouri— "Show Me"—to portray the Gulch as a challenge: "show me; prove to me that you can get to the top." It was a challenge! In just over a half mile, we had to climb five thousand feet. The climb was virtually straight up. However, the real challenge was not that one climb, but what was beyond, because when we had clawed our way to the top of Missouri Gulch, there were still more mountains to climb!

Life is that way! There are many different levels in life which we experience as we climb to the Mountaintop of Praise. First, there is the level which is exhilarating, ecstatic, jubilant, and joyful. Isaiah referred to this level when he wrote, "they shall mount up with wings like eagles."[291] When the Israelites had been freed from their slavery in Egypt, and God opened the Red Sea and delivered them from the Egyptian army, they had experienced this exhilaration of freedom. Later, when they entered the Promised Land, they again experienced the triumphant thrill of God's fulfilled promises. A similar moment of ecstasy was experienced by the Jewish people who returned to Jerusalem in 538 BC from their seventy years of captivity in Babylonia.

The New Testament records similar parallel experiences. The widow of Nain knew the joy of "mounting up with wings of ea-

---

[291] Isaiah 40:31

gles" as the Lord Jesus raised her only son from death.

Bartimaeus and the lepers leaped for joy when Jesus healed them. Peter, James, and John, the disciples of Jesus, walked on this level when they were on the Mount of Transfiguration with Jesus. Again, on Resurrection Sunday, the disciples knew the thrill of triumph when Jesus appeared to them in the Upper Room.

All of us have experienced such times of "mounting up with wings like eagles" when we have jubilantly raised our arms in a Rocky Balboa-like victory salute. During those times, we felt that God was right by our side. Those times are valid, and we should live them out to the fullest. We must remember, however, that not all life is lived on the mountaintop. There are times when we walk in the valleys and do not experience God's presence. We do not "mount up with wings"; instead, we struggle as we seek strength to walk on the path of life.

Isaiah then refers to a second level of life: "They will run and not get tired."[292] This level refers to the endurance an athlete needs when he competes in an event. Runners know there is a point in a long run when they hit the wall. It is a point when it seems as if the runner cannot take another step. The wall is simply too much to overcome! All the runner can do is to force himself or herself to take one more step, and then another and then another. With determination and focus, the runner eventually breaks through the wall of fatigue and continues the race to the end.

Many times, we hit the wall in life when we do not think we can

---

[292] Isaiah 40:31

continue. The daily affairs of life seem so overwhelming. Like the runner, we must take one more step of faith and then another and then another. God promises He will strengthen and enable us to continue the climb.

One of the ways to overcome the walls of life is to stay busy, to be so involved with the daily affairs of life that there is no opportunity for despair. Activity forces our attention off our difficulties and redirects our efforts into other areas of life.

After a great victory over the false prophets of Baal,[293] the Hebrew prophet Elijah hit the wall. Threatened by the wicked Queen Jezebel who sought revenge for the death of her prophets, Elijah "was afraid and ran for his life." In utter despair, Elijah asked God to "take his life."[294] Instead God sent the prophet on a forty-day journey to Horeb, the mountain of God. There God revealed himself to Elijah[295] much as He revealed Himself to Habakkuk.[296] Rather than allow Elijah to wallow in his despair, God sent him back into spiritual warfare against the wicked Ahab and Jezebel. Like Elijah and Isaiah and Habakkuk, we must run through the walls of adversity!

During the experience with his daughter's struggle against leukemia, John Claypool hit the wall many times. Reflecting on those times, Claypool recalls: "I plunged headlong into what had to be faced."[297] His busy schedule as a pastor enabled him to run through the wall of despair which was always present at the edge

---

[293] 1 Kings 18
[294] 1 Kings 19:1–4
[295] 1 Kings 19:9–15
[296] Habakkuk 3
[297] Claypool, *Fellow Struggler,* 30.

of his mind. Throughout my own years of ministry, many people have related to me that if it were not for their work, they would go out of their mind worrying about difficulties. It is in those moments we must follow Habakkuk's example and patiently "wait on the Lord to gain new strength."

Undoubtedly, there are times in life when we cannot "mount up with wings," and we cannot run. Sometimes the mountains of life are so steep and rough that we are forced to a walk. The challenges of life become an unbearable burden. Matters are so difficult that we can go on only by taking just one step at a time.

The prophet Isaiah refers to this third level of life: "They will walk and not become weary."[298] How? How does a person "not become weary" in such times? How does he or she get through the wall in such times? The answer lies in Isaiah's earlier words: "Do you not know? Have you not heard? Yahweh is the everlasting God, the creator of the whole earth. He never grows faint or weary; there is no limit to His understanding. He gives strength to the weary and strengthens the powerless."[299] Isaiah's message is clear. Our strength and endurance come from God, not from ourselves. In such times, we simply hang on and walk by faith in God. Remember God's words to Habakkuk: "The righteous will live by his faith."[300] The apostle Paul proclaimed: "God will not allow us to be tested beyond what we are able, but with the trial will also provide a way of escape, that we may be able to endure it."[301] As someone aptly phrased it: "keep on keeping on." We must walk on

---

[298]   Isaiah 40:31
[299]   Isaiah 40:28–29
[300]   Habakkuk 2:4
[301]   1 Corinthians 10:13

regardless of the circumstances!

Habakkuk relates his experience of hitting the wall in the last few verses of his book. God had told him that the future held only destruction, famine, sorrow, and death for the people of Israel. Habakkuk's "inward parts trembled, his lips quivered, and decay entered his bones." He could do nothing except "wait quietly for the day of distress."[302] Even as his world collapsed around him, and the way to the top of the mountain seemed hopeless, Habakkuk acted in an astounding way. Listen to his words: "Yet, I will exult in the Lord, I will rejoice in the God of my salvation. The Lord God is my strength; He has made my feet like hinds' feet; and, He makes me walk on my high places."[303]

Instead of becoming despondent and bitter, Habakkuk began to praise the Lord. Even in his despair, the prophet cried out in victory. We wonder, "How could he rejoice in such circumstances?" First, he *waited on the Lord and gained new strength.* He was willing to trust God to work out His will on His timetable.[304] This is the life of faith that God calls us to live. We must remember that God sees the big picture. We see only the present moment in which we are living. While the present moment may be dark, difficult, and daunting, God sees what lies beyond the present and knows the ultimate outcome. It is the "waiting on the Lord" that will enable us to move beyond the present and experience His tomorrow.

When the Jews returned to Israel after their seventy years of

[302] Habakkuk 3:16
[303] Habakkuk 3:18–19
[304] Habakkuk 2:3

captivity in Babylon, they faced trials on every side. The land was desolate, they were harassed by surrounding enemy nations, and God seemed to be silent. During these difficult times, as they tried to rebuild the razed walls of Jerusalem and the Temple, Ezra the priest spoke these words of encouragement to the people: "Do not grieve, because your strength comes from rejoicing in the LORD."[305] Centuries earlier the psalmist had written, "This is the day that the Lord has made. Let us rejoice and be glad in it."[306] Nothing ever happens in life which is beyond and outside the knowledge and power of God. He will always be there for us, even in the darkest valleys; He will lead us along the rough and crooked paths; and, His goodness and faithful love will pursue us.[307]

Second, Habakkuk remembered who God is.[308] He remembered that God is the Creator, the Giver, the Sustainer, and the Controller of all life. Everything belongs to Him, and He gives everything—even life—to us as a gift. The proper way to treat a gift is with gratitude. Even if the gift is taken from us, we should still be grateful to God that He had given us the gift for a period. Even as he was losing everything precious in his life, Habakkuk still rejoiced in the Lord.

This attitude of gratitude will sustain a person during tragedy, such as the death of a child, a spouse, a parent, or a friend. The pain and the sorrow will still be present, and rightly so, because we are people of emotions. Yet as we rejoice and thank God for the gift of life which He gave to us for a moment, we live by

---

[305] Nehemiah 8:10
[306] Psalm 118:24
[307] Psalm 23
[308] Habakkuk 3:3–15

faith in God. This is what the apostle Paul meant when he wrote: "Rejoice always; pray without ceasing; in everything give thanks; for this is God's will for you in Christ Jesus."[309] It was this attitude of gratitude which sustained Habakkuk. It was this attitude of gratitude which sustained John Claypool as he experienced the death of his daughter.[310] It was this attitude of gratitude that I had to learn when my son was killed in the War on Terror! It is this attitude of gratitude that will sustain all of God's children in their difficult moments of life.

Third, the prophet remembered the great works of deliverance of the Israelites by God in the past. Habakkuk's third vision from God contains numerous references to the ways God delivered the Israelites out of slavery in Egypt. He had sustained the people for forty years as they wandered in the wilderness. In the end, God had destroyed their enemies in Canaan and had given them the land just as He had promised. Habakkuk remembered God was "unchanging and that His ways are everlasting."[311] When his world was collapsing, the prophet knew he could depend on God. He trusted God would be an anchor that he could hold onto during the storm.

Like Habakkuk, we live in a world of constant change: a world in which there seems to be no absolutes, and nothing exists on which a person can depend. Like the prophet, we must remember that God can be depended on. He never changes, He will never forsake us, and He is an anchor which will always hold firm in the

---

[309]   1 Thessalonians 5:16–18
[310]   Claypool, *Fellow Struggler,* 79.
[311]   Habakkuk 3:6

most violent storm. Listen to these words of hope from the psalm-ist: "Sing praise to the Lord, you His godly ones, and give thanks to His holy name: for His anger is but for a moment, His favor is for a life time. Weeping may last for the night, but a shout of joy comes in the morning."[312] Like Habakkuk, we need to let the Lord God be our strength. I pray you will experience the shout of joy in the morning in your life as you wait quietly on the Lord. He will enable you to reach the Mountaintop of Praise.

REFLECTIONS

1. What does it mean to "wait on the Lord"?

2. Explain a time in your life when you "mounted up with wings like eagles."

3. Describe a time in your life when you hit the wall. How did you overcome the wall?

4. In a world of constant change, how do you maintain stability in your life?

---

[312] Psalm 30:4-5

*The way to deal with stress
is to acknowledge God
and allow Him to grant
healing and refreshment.*

CHAPTER TWELVE
WALK ON

The LORD is my strength,
"And He has made my feet like hinds' feet,
And makes me walk on my high places.

HABAKKUK 3:19

Earlier I mentioned my climb of Mount Fuji while stationed in Japan as an Air Force Academy cadet. Since the climb is designed to reach the top of Mount Fuji shortly before dawn so you see the magnificent beauty of the sunrise, the climb takes place at night. The climb is long and tiring. About two-thirds of the way up the mountain, a stop is made at a small lodge to rest. We slept on Japanese bamboo mats for about three hours, and the rest was greatly needed. When I am exhausted, I can sleep on anything!

The climb is not only tiring; it is also dangerous. The path is narrow and twists and turns back and forth across the face of the mountain. Each person carried a torch to light the path, and the tour guides continually reminded us not to stray off the path. At one point, I discovered why! We had stopped for a five-minute rest, and I took a couple of steps to my right. One of the tour guides hollered and grabbed me. He thrust his torch in front of me and pointed downward. A deep chasm lay beneath my feet. It must have been a thousand feet straight down! I never moved one inch off the path the rest of the climb. Despite the danger and the weariness, when we reached the top and the sun rose over the horizon, the sight was beyond description. No artist could paint such awesome beauty. The climb was worth every step!

The closing verses of Habakkuk's book are similar. The prophet had walked a long and treacherous path from the Valley of Despair to the Mountaintop of Praise. Along the journey, he had needed several rest stops of prayer and meditation. There were times when he had almost fallen off the path of faith.

Through God's visions, the prophet experienced the coming days of distress. He watched as his people and the city of Jerusalem were destroyed, as the land was devastated, and the animals slaughtered. Like the guide on Mount Fuji, God had continually kept the prophet safe. Finally, the dawn came, and the prophet saw the splendor and radiance of God cover the heavens, just as I saw the beauty of the sunrise from the top of Mount Fuji.

Habakkuk had finished his journey of life and faith; he had completed his climb from the Valley of Despair to the Mountaintop of Praise. His words for us are like the anchor of a ship which holds a ship secure during a storm. Pay close attention to what he declares; there are three final lessons for us to learn from the prophet.

First, during the storm, Habakkuk declared: "Yahweh is my strength."[313] *The great and awesome "I AM" was always there for Habakkuk. He is always there for us!* He is "Whatever We Need Him to Be." No evil can overcome us, because He is the Almighty Power. Yes, we will become weary and faint, and we will stumble badly, but "those who wait on Him will gain new strength."[314] We make a mistake, and our troubles are compounded when we depend upon our own strength, our own wisdom, and our own abilities. As mentioned earlier, we are like the small child who says, "I do it."

In 2013, I taught a class of sophomores who were outstanding in so many ways—in the academic classroom and on the athletic fields. There were also several of them who continually comment-

---

[313] Habakkuk 3:19a
[314] Isaiah 40:30–31

ed, "I'm so stressed! I'm so stressed!" One young lady gained notoriety among her classmates to the point they prayed daily that she might experience "compassionate fatigue" (their code words for God to heal her stress).

Many of us have the same need! Like Habakkuk, we need to let God be our strength. As the Ancient Teacher wrote: "Acknowledge Him … it will be healing to your body and refreshment to your bones."[315] Interestingly, the young lady wrote a paper at the end of the course on the topic of stress. She had learned that the way to deal with stress was to acknowledge God and allow Him to grant her healing and refreshment.

In the movie *Chariots of Fire,* Eric Liddell is running a race when he is knocked off his feet and lands on the infield of the track. As you watch the scene, he lies on the ground as the others race down the track. Then, almost in slow motion, Liddell pushes himself to his feet and races after the runners ahead of him. He passes one, then another and another and another. At the finish line, he surges ahead and breaks the tape to win the race. Where did his strength come from? In Liddell's words, it came from God who "increases power."[316] That same power is available to us!

Second, the prophet declares: "He has made my feet like hind's feet."[317] Habakkuk makes an interesting analogy with these words. The hind [deer] is an extremely sure-footed animal and easily runs and climbs difficult and craggy terrain during all types of weather and all times of day and night. The prophet understands it is God's

---

[315] Proverbs 3:6, 8
[316] Isaiah 40:29
[317] Habakkuk 3:19b

wisdom that enables him to overcome the difficult obstacles of life. He acknowledges it is God who guides him along the demanding journey of life and gives him sure-footedness so he does not fall.

Like Habakkuk, we need to allow God to give us "hind's feet" and show us how to walk on the heights of our journey of life and faith. Isaiah, the Prince of Prophets, who preceded Habakkuk by 125 years, spoke similar words of advice: "Whether you turn to the right or to the left, your ears will hear a voice behind you, saying, 'This is the way; walk in it.'"[318]

Third, Habakkuk proclaims, "And, God makes me walk on my high places."[319] With these last words, the prophet stands at the head of a long line of Christian men and women who through the centuries of history have completed and won the race of life. The phrase "my high places" points to the raised platform on which the victor of a race is awarded the trophy or crown of victory.

In the New Testament, the apostle Paul speaks of this same victorious event: "Do you not know that those who run in a race all run, but only one receives the prize? Run in such a way that you may win."[320] In a letter to the Christians in Philippi, Paul writes, "I press on toward the goal to win the prize for which God has called me heavenward in Christ Jesus."[321] Near the end of his life and while in prison Paul pens these final words to the young pastor Timothy: "I have fought the good fight; I have finished the

[318]   Isaiah 30:21
[319]   Habakkuk 3:19c
[320]   1 Corinthians 9:24
[321]   Philippians 3:14

race; and, I have kept the faith. Now there is in store for me the crown of righteousness, which the Lord, the righteous Judge, will award to me on that day."[322] Both the prophet Habakkuk and the apostle Paul, separated by six hundred years, walked on their high places of victory.

Most of us have probably seen the award ceremonies at the Olympics on TV. We have watched as the victors stood on the raised platforms with their faces wreathed in joy and satisfaction as they receive their medals. For many years, they had worked hard, and now their disciplined training has enabled them to achieve this highest goal in the athletic world. From the beginning to the end of his book, the prophet Habakkuk had run the race of life and faith. Listen to the words of God to him: "Record the vision and inscribe it on tablets, the one who reads it may run. For the vision is yet for the appointed time; it hastens toward the goal, and it will not fail. Though it tarries, wait for it; for it will certainly come, it will not delay."[323] Habakkuk had lived by faith through-out his long and difficult journey from the Valley of Despair to the Mountaintop of Praise, and at the end, God awarded him the victor's crown on the high places of glory.

What a powerful ending to this ancient book—short in length, but long in encouragement! I do not know where you are on your journey of life and faith, but I challenge you to read these words of Habakkuk, not once, but many times. I challenge you to hear and heed the prophet's words so that you too may stand on the high

---

[322] 2 Timothy 4:7
[323] Habakkuk 2:2–3

places and receive from God your crown of victory. I challenge you to walk on in faith regardless of the circumstances you face in life.

In closing, heed these words of the author of the New Testament book of Hebrews, words which convey the same truths of Habakkuk: "Therefore, since we have so great a cloud of witnesses surrounding us, let us also lay aside every encumbrance, and the sin which so easily entangles us, and let us run with endurance the race that is set before us."[324] Life and faith is a journey; enjoy it! You will never regret it!

REFLECTIONS

1. Is stress a major factor in your daily life?

2. How do you resolve the stress?

3. What factors in your life enable you to "walk on high places"?

---

[324] Hebrews 12:1

*We cannot turn our eyes
only upon the wonders
of the mountaintop.
We must also look upon
the depths of the valley below.*

Afterword

The righteous will live by faith.

HABAKKUK 2:4

Well, the journey is over—not really. It is just beginning! Even when we reach the Mountaintop of Praise, we still have much that lies ahead of us. We cannot turn our eyes only upon the wonders of the mountaintop. We must also look upon the depths of the valley below. It is easy to live by faith when we are on the mountaintop, it is challenging to live by faith when we are in the valley. Moses knew that. Joseph knew that. Habakkuk knew that. Peter knew that. Paul knew that. And, yes, even Jesus knew that.

A story is recorded in three of the four New Testament gospels which teach us this truth.[325] The story has two parts. The first part reveals the glories of God which we find on the mountain- top. The second part reveals the challenges of life we will find in the depths of the valley below. The disciples of Jesus had to learn this truth. So do we!

The story is the account of the Transfiguration of Jesus as witnessed by three of Jesus' disciples—Peter, James, and John. The event occurred in the third and final year of Jesus' ministry. The first two years were Jesus' years of popularity. Great

---

[325] Matthew 17:1–20; Mark 9:2–8; Luke 9:28–36

crowds followed Him everywhere as He taught, performed miracles, and healed the sick. These two years were exciting times. In many people's minds, the Old Testament prophecies and prayers for the Messiah to come had been fulfilled. The disciples of Jesus felt they were walking on the mountaintop of life.

During the first two years of Jesus' ministry, the political and religious leaders had occasionally questioned Him as they sought to understand who He was. In the third year of His ministry, opposition intensified and hardened against Jesus. Deliberate confrontations with the religious leaders became common, and specific plans were made to kill Jesus.[326] Many of His followers turned away and no longer walked with Jesus. His teachings had become "hard and unacceptable."[327]

During this increased opposition, the Transfiguration of Jesus occurred.[328] One wonders why it took place now. Why did John, who observed the event, not write about it in his Gospel? What is its significance? I believe the answers lie in the great lesson of faith which Jesus taught the twelve disciples. It is possible that the lesson led to the eventual betrayal by Judas. The lesson was, and still is, hard!

First, all of us like to be on the mountaintops of life. We enjoy those times when everything is going well in our lives— when there are no obstacles to confront, when the high fives and pats-on-the-back are experienced and expressed. Like the

---

[326]   John 5:16; 7:1
[327]   John 6:60–68
[328]   Matthew 17:1–8

TV program, such times are truly "Happy Days." We relish the victories, the championships, the trophies.

Peter, James, and John experienced this joy as they witnessed the many miracles performed by Jesus. The Transfiguration had to have been an exhilarating time! To see the magnificent glory of Jesus and to listen to Him talk with Moses and Elijah must have been the mountaintop of their walk with Jesus. Little wonder Peter wanted to build three tabernacles and stay on the top of the mountain. It would have been easy to live by faith in such surroundings! However, Jesus' lesson was not finished.

During the second part of the lesson Jesus took the disciples into the valley below.[329] Unless the lesson was completed, He knew the disciples would have been left with only a little faith, a faith good enough for mountaintop living, but not for valley living.

In the valley, a father had brought his epileptic son to the disciples to heal. Remember Jesus had earlier "given the disciples authority to cast out unclean spirits and to heal every kind of disease and every kind of sickness."[330] Then, they had been successful.[331] Now "they could not cure the boy."[332] When the disciples asked Jesus, "Why could we not cast the demon out?" He replied, "Because of the littleness of your faith."[333] There is a difference between faith on the mountaintop and faith in the valley. What is the difference?

---

[329] Matthew 17:9–20
[330] Matthew 10:1
[331] Mark 6:13
[332] Matthew 17:16
[333] Matthew 17:20

On the mountaintop, we live by our emotions. In the valley, we must live by God's spirit of faith. If we examine the words of God to Habakkuk, we discover this truth: "Behold, as for the proud one, his soul is not right within him. But the righteous will live by his faith."[334] To live by faith is to live a righteous life, to obey God's commandments and ways, to follow in Jesus' footsteps, to experience God as the beginning and the end of our life.

Paul proclaimed the same truth in two of his epistles, as did the writer of the book of Hebrews: it is only the righteous who live by faith.[335] Habakkuk understood this truth as he "waited quietly for the day of distress"[336] and depended upon Yahweh as his strength. The disciples learned this truth in the valley, and it sustained them in the years after Jesus' ascension. We, too, must learn and practice this lesson in our lives. May our prayer be that of the disciples: "Lord, increase our faith!"[337] Walk on ... by faith!

Thus, says the LORD,
"Call unto Me,
And I will answer you;
And, I will show you great and mighty things,
Which you do not know.

JEREMIAH 33:3

---

[334] Habakkuk 2:4
[335] Romans 1:17; Galatians 3:12; Hebrews: 10:38–39
[336] Habakkuk 3:16
[337] Luke 17:5

BIBLIOGRAPHY

Blackaby, Henry. *Experiencing God Study*. Nashville: B & H Publishing Group, 1990.

Bullock, C. Hassell. *An Introduction to the Old Testament Prophetic Books*. Chicago: Moody Publishers, 1986.

Buttrick, George Arthur. *The Interpreter's Bible*, Vol. VI, *"The Book of Habakkuk,"* by Charles L. Taylor, Jr. and Howard Thurman. New York and Nashville: Abingdon Press, 1956.

Center for Disease Control and Prevention, *"Alcohol Drinking Statistics."* cdc.gov/nchs/fastats/alcohol.htm.

Chambers, Oswald. *My Utmost for His Highest*. New York: Dodd, Mead & Company, 1935.

Claypool, John. *The Tracks of a Fellow Struggler*. New York: Church Publishing Inc., 2004.

Damon, Arwa. *"Bringing Babylon Back from the Dead."* CNN. April 4, 2013.

Davidson, A. B. *The Books of Nahum, Habakkuk, and Zephaniah*. Cambridge: University Press, 1920.

Dostoevsky, Fyodor. *The Brothers Karamozov.* Trans. Richard Pevear and Larissa Volokhonsky. New York: Farrar, Straus and Giroux, 1990.

Evett, Marianne B. *"Feast of the Transfiguration."* A Sermon delivered at All Saints Parish, Brookline, Massachusetts. August 4-5, 2007.

Freeman, Hobart E. *An Introduction to the Old Testament Prophets.* Chicago: Moody Press, 1981.

Gaebelein, Frank E. *Four Minor Prophets: Their Message for Today.* Chicago: Moody Press, 1970.

Geisler, Norman L. *Christian Ethics.* Grand Rapids, Michigan: Baker Academic, 2nd Edition, 2010.

Golding, William. *Lord of the Flies.* New York: Coward, McCann & Geoghegan, Inc., 1954.

Harris, R. Laird, and Gleason L. Archer, Jr., and Bruce I. Waltke, Eds. *Theological Wordbook of the Old Testament.* 2 vols. Chicago: Moody Press, 1980.

Harrison, R. K. *Introduction to the Old Testament.* Grand Rapids: Eerdmans, 1969.

Heflin, J. N. Boo. *Nahum, Habakkuk, Zephaniah, and Haggai.* Grand Rapids: Lamplighter Books, 1985.

Heschel, Abraham J. *The Prophets.* Vol. 1. New York: Harper and Row, Publishers, 1962.

Hunter, John E. *Major Truths from the Minor Prophets*. Grand Rapids: Zondervan Publishing House, 1978.

Huey, F. B., Jr. *Yesterday's Prophets for Today's World*. Nashville: Broadman Press, 1980.

Isaacs, Stan. "*Bud's Olympiads Are Worth Their Weight in Gold*." Newsday. 5 Nov. 1991.

Lindblom, J. *Prophecy in Ancient Israel*. Philadelphia: Fortress Press, 1962.

Lloyd-Jones, D. Martyn. *From Fear to Faith: Studies in the Book of Habakkuk*. Grand Rapids: Baker Book House, 1982.

Mullins, Rich. "*My Deliverer*," in *The Jesus Record*. By Songwriters Chad Robert Cates, Tony W. Wood, Jason Walker. Word Entertainment, July 21, 1998.

National Institute on Alcohol Abuse and Alcoholism. "*Alcohol Facts and Statistics*." pubs.niaaa.nih.gov.

Pusey, E. B. *The Minor Prophets*, Vol. 2. Grand Rapids, MI: Baker Book House, 1978.

Rand, Ayn. *Atlas Shrugged*. New York: Random House, 1957.

Russell, Bertrand. "*Why I Am Not a Christian*." Why I Am Not a Christian and Other Essays on Religion and Related Subjects. Ed. Paul Edwards. New York: Simon and Schuster, 1967.

Schaeffer, Frances. *He Is There, and He Is Not Silent*. Wheaton, IL: Tyndale House Publishers, 1972.

Scott, R. B. Y. *The Relevance of the Prophets*. New York: The
    Macmillian Company, 1944.

Sire, James W. *The Universe Next Door.* Downers Grove, Illinois:
    IVP Academic, 2009.

Sorrell, Sammy. *Home Grown Terrorism.* Albuquerque, New
    Mexico: American Trend Publishing, 2006.

"*The Bible: Can We Trust It?*" Rapture Ready. August 8, 2016 by
    RR@admin2.   www.raptureready.com/rr-bible.html.

Tolkien, J.R.R. *The Fellowship of the Ring*, First edition, London:
    George Allen & Unwin 1954, Second edition, Boston:
    Houghton Mifflin, 1967.

"*Top 10 Emotional Olympic Moments*," (ListVerse, December
    6, 2009), http://listverse.com/2009/12/06/top-10-emotional-
    olympic-moments

U2. "*Walk On*," in *All That You Can't Leave Behind.* Island/Inter
    Scope Records, November 2001. CD

Ungerer, Walter J. *Habakkuk: The Man with Honest Questions*.
    Grand Rapids: Baker Book House, 1976.

VanGemeren, William A. *Interpreting the Prophetic Word*. Grand
    Rapids: Zondervan Publishing House, 1990.

"*We'll See*." Author unknown. Inspiration Peak. http://www.
    inspirationpeak.com/cgi-bin/stories.cgi?record=31.

Welland, Colin. *Chariots of Fire*. Film. Directed by Hugh Hudson.
    Century City, Los Angeles, CA: 20th Century Fox, 1981.

Yancey, Phillip. *Disappointment with God*. Grand Rapids: Zondervan Publishing House, 1988.

Young, Edward J. *My Servants the Prophets*. Grand Rapids: Wm. B. Eerdmans Publishing Company, 1952.

Young, Robert. *Analytical Concordance to the Bible*. Grand Rapids: Wm. B. Eerdmans Publishing Company, 1970.

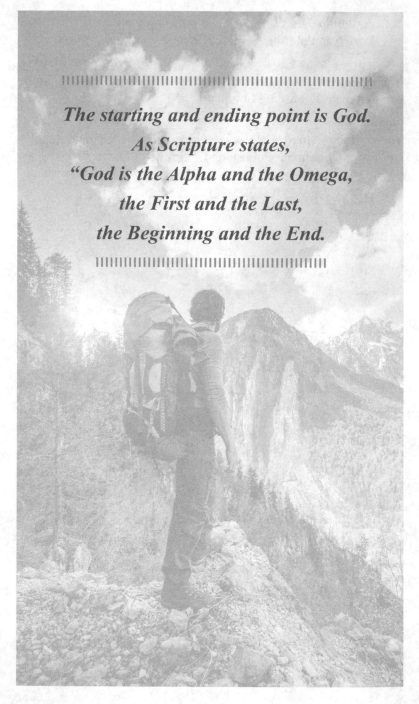

The starting and ending point is God.
As Scripture states,
"God is the Alpha and the Omega,
the First and the Last,
the Beginning and the End.

Acknowledgments

I suspect many authors find the acknowledgments to be the most difficult portion of a book to write. How does one acknowledge all the people who have influenced the author as he or she has written a book? Where does one start, and where does one end?

For me, the starting and ending point is God. As Scripture states, "God is the Alpha and the Omega, the First and the Last, the Beginning and the End."[338] From that point, the list becomes almost limitless.

The most obvious are my parents, Richard and Nora Bracy, who sacrificed their lives to give me life. My mother was my first school teacher and taught me to seek and live truth wherever it was to be found. My father taught me grace and discipline as he guided me along the path of life. My many family relatives—grandparents, aunts and uncles, and cousins—and the larger community family of Bethesda, Arkansas, showed me the value of personal relationships.

The many teachers and coaches I had from elementary school through college mentored me as I explored the intellectual halls of knowledge and challenged the physical arenas of athletics. Classmates and teammates provided friendship and empathy

---

[338] Revelation 22:13

as we enjoyed—and sometimes cried over—our childhood, teenage, and college years.

Fellow airmen, soldiers, and sailors shared forty-two years of military life with its demands, fears, loneliness, and sacrifices. Some gave the ultimate sacrifice of life; others endured the harrows of captivity and imprisonment. But all of us experienced the unique camaraderie which only warriors fully know. We were a band of brothers forged in the fires of battle. Two of these were Michael Bevaque and John Stockreiser, with whom I flew over 1,800 hours in the RF-4C as we faced the dangers of war. Two other comrades-in-arms, Darrell Highsmith and Ray Kilgore, were commanders and friends. They taught me how to be both a warrior and a Christian.

In the world of academia, Dr. Boo Heflin is foremost. He was my major professor during my masters and PhD studies and a demanding taskmaster—six months just to approve the title of my dissertation! Dr. Jimmie Nelson and Dr. F. B. Huey, Jr., read and edited and edited and edited the Habakkuk manuscript; I am grateful for their relentless diligence. They ensured the content and meaning of the text were accurate and understandable.

One other person was a joy to work with during the development of this book: Miss Lauren Robertson, one of my students at San Antonio Christian Schools (SACS). Miss Robertson was an outstanding student and an editor of the school magazine. She spent the summer between her sophomore and junior years of high school proofreading the manuscript, and she was a tough editor.

Her insights from an ordinary young adult reader's perspective were invaluable. Two other students of mine at SACS used their gifts of artistry to visually portray the journey of life and faith. Mr. Grant Leslie designed the initial cover of the book, and Miss Amy Mireles drew the vivid sketches which illustrate the book.

The communities of San Antonio Christian Schools (SACS) and Geneva Classical and Christian School of Boerne (GSB) played a significant role in the writing of this book. Alan Axtell, superintendent, and Rob Armstrong, principal (SACS), and Brad Ryden, Head of School, and John DeSario, Headmaster of Logic School (GSB), looked beyond the box of traditions and gave me an opportunity to fulfill God's will and teach at SACS and GSB. Colleagues, both teachers and coaches, were sources of wisdom and encouragement as we entered daily into the lives of the students and athletes at SACS and GSB. Thank you for walking with me on this journey.

I must acknowledge one other group who has had a major role in the writing of this book: the people of the churches where I was pastor; the members of the military units I served in; and, the students I have taught in secondary schools, colleges, and graduate schools. I walked through many long and challenging roads of life with them. Beyond a doubt, I learned much from them which is embedded in *Walk On*.

I thank the owner and publisher of Carpenter's Son Publishers, Larry Carpenter; the book cover and interior design editor, Debbie Manning Sheppard; and the copy editor, Gail Fallen, who have guided me through the printing of this book. They have graciously endured my many questions and have enriched the content in numerous ways so that you will hopefully have an enjoyable reading and learning experience.

Finally, I thank and appreciate my wife of fifty years, Judith, and my children, Tonya and Todd, for your love and support as I wrote this book. You are the core of my life here on Earth, and you gave much of yourselves to allow me the time to write. Your lives and love are written into each letter and every word of this book.

I pray God's blessings on all who have participated, knowingly and unknowingly, in this project. May you experience the fullness of life and faith as you *Walk On*.

May you experience the fullness of life and faith as you

WALK ON

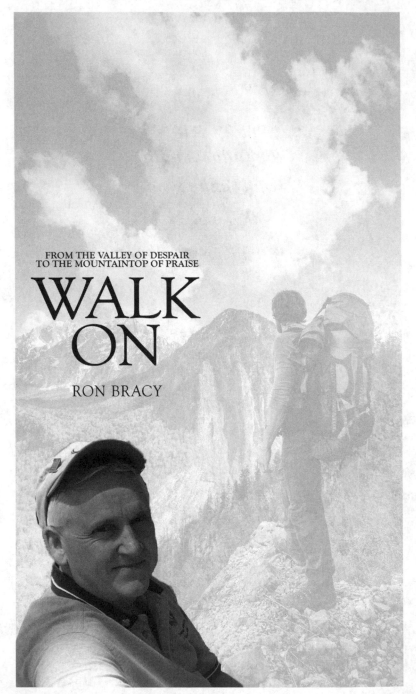

FROM THE VALLEY OF DESPAIR
TO THE MOUNTAINTOP OF PRAISE

WALK ON

RON BRACY

About the Author

DR. RON BRACY was born at an Army hospital in Fort Monmouth, New Jersey, on December 3, 1944. He lived in Aurora, Illinois, and Borger, Texas, with his mother and grandparents during his early years. At the age of five, he was adopted by his aunt and uncle, Nora and Richard Bracy, and grew up in Bethesda, Arkansas. During his childhood and teenage years, the seed of God's Word was planted deeply in his life by his parents and the people of a small rural Baptist church. They taught him to seek the Truth, a desire which still drives his life.

Upon graduation from high school in Batesville, Arkansas, Dr. Bracy entered the US Air Force Academy in Colorado Springs, Colorado, planning a career in the military. He graduated in 1966 with a bachelor's degree in humanities and served forty-two years in the Active, Reserve, and National Guard components of the Air Force in numerous countries and situations around the world. During his military career, he received numerous federal and state military and civilian awards in recognition of his service to our country.

In the Vietnam War (1968–69) he flew 183 combat missions (101 over North Vietnam). Returning from the war, Dr. Bracy was haunted by the question, "Why did I live and others die?" Other events such as the death of his parents, 9/11—he was on duty at the Pentagon when the terrorists crashed the airplane into the building—two personal life-threatening illnesses, and the seemingly meaninglessness of life itself in a chaotic world eventually brought him face-to-face with his own mortality and lead him on a search for the reality of God. In the German town of Zweibrucken ("Two Bridges"), on the night of July 24, 1970, he finally found the Truth and peace for which he had searched for many years—Jesus Christ.

In time Dr. Bracy left the military world and entered the academic world in 1976. He earned master's and PhD degrees in biblical studies and ethics from Southwestern Baptist Theological Seminary. Upon graduation from seminary, he served as a pastor, a reserve military chaplain, and a teacher. He has taught at all levels of education including secondary schools, colleges, and graduate schools, and currently teaches Old Testament and Historical Theology at Geneva Classical and Christian School in Boerne, Texas. He has been a guest speaker for conferences, seminars, and civic events and has written at all levels of academia. He also completed a course for writers at Long Ridge Writers Group and has had one article series published. His PhD dissertation is on file at the Library of Congress. He can be contacted via email at **walkonministries@gmail.com** and the web site **walkonministries.my-free.website.**

Dr. Bracy and his wife Judith live in San Antonio, Texas. Their daughter and her family live nearby, as does their daughter-in-law and her family. They enjoy their lives as grandparents and spend as much time as possible with their five grandchildren and four great-grandchildren.

At a museum in Fort Worth, Texas, Dr. Bracy once read these words: "A building under construction is never completed." Those words reflect his view of the Christian journey of life and faith. He is still learning how to *Walk On*.

||||||||||||||||||||||||||||||||||||||||||||||||||||||||||||

"A building under construction
is never completed."
These words reflect
Ron's view of the Christian
journey of life and faith.

||||||||||||||||||||||||||||||||||||||||||||||||||||

Habakkuk 1
New American Standard Bible (NASB)

Chaldeans Used to Punish Judah

1 The oracle which Habakkuk the prophet saw.

2   How long, O Lord, will I call for help,
And You will not hear?
I cry out to You, "Violence!"
Yet You do not save.

3   Why do You make me see iniquity,
And cause me to look on wickedness?
Yes, destruction and violence are before me;
Strife exists and contention arises.

4   Therefore the law is ignored
And justice is never upheld.
For the wicked surround the righteous;
Therefore justice comes out perverted.

5   "Look among the nations! Observe!
Be astonished! Wonder!
Because I am doing something in your days—
You would not believe if you were told.

6   "For behold, I am raising up the Chaldeans,
That fierce and impetuous people
Who march throughout the earth
To seize dwelling places which are not theirs.

7   "They are dreaded and feared;
Their justice and authority originate with themselves.

8   "Their horses are swifter than leopards
And keener than wolves in the evening.
Their horsemen come galloping,

Their horsemen come from afar;
They fly like an eagle swooping down to devour.

9   "All of them come for violence.
Their horde of faces moves forward.
They collect captives like sand.

10 "They mock at kings
And rulers are a laughing matter to them.
They laugh at every fortress
And heap up rubble to capture it.

11 "Then they will sweep through like the wind and pass on.
But they will be held guilty,
They whose strength is their god."

12 Are You not from everlasting,
O Lord, my God, my Holy One?
We will not die.
You, O Lord, have appointed them to judge;
And You, O Rock, have established them to correct.

13 Your eyes are too pure to approve evil,
And You can not look on wickedness with favor.
Why do You look with favor
On those who deal treacherously?
Why are You silent when the wicked swallow up
Those more righteous than they?

14 Why have You made men like the fish of the sea,
Like creeping things without a ruler over them?

15 The Chaldeans bring all of them up with a hook,
Drag them away with their net,
And gather them together in their fishing net.
Therefore they rejoice and are glad.

16 Therefore they offer a sacrifice to their net
And burn incense to their fishing net;
Because through these things their catch is large,
And their food is plentiful.

17 Will they therefore empty their net
And continually slay nations without sparing?

Habakkuk 2
New American Standard Bible (NASB)

God Answers the Prophet

1   I will stand on my guard post
And station myself on the rampart;
And I will keep watch to see what He will speak to me,
And how I may reply when I am reproved.

2   Then the Lord answered me and said,
"Record the vision
And inscribe it on tablets,
That the one who reads it may run

.3   "For the vision is yet for the appointed time;
It hastens toward the goal and it will not fail.
Though it tarries, wait for it;
For it will certainly come, it will not delay.

4   "Behold, as for the proud one,
His soul is not right within him;
But the righteous will live by his faith.

5   "Furthermore, wine betrays the haughty man,
So that he does not stay at home.
He enlarges his appetite like Sheol,
And he is like death, never satisfied.
He also gathers to himself all nations
And collects to himself all peoples.

6   "Will not all of these take up a taunt-song against him,
Even mockery and insinuations against him
And say, 'Woe to him who increases what is not his—
For how long—

And makes himself rich with loans?'

7   "Will not your creditors rise up suddenly,
    And those who collect from you awaken?
    Indeed, you will become plunder for them.

8   "Because you have looted many nations,
    All the remainder of the peoples will loot you—
    Because of human bloodshed and violence done to the land,
    To the town and all its inhabitants.

9   "Woe to him who gets evil gain for his house
    To put his nest on high,
    To be delivered from the hand of calamity!

10 "You have devised a shameful thing for your house
    By cutting off many peoples;
    So you are sinning against yourself.

11 "Surely the stone will cry out from the wall,
    And the rafter will answer it from the [k]framework.

12 "Woe to him who builds a city with bloodshed
    And founds a town with violence!

13 "Is it not indeed from the Lord of hosts
    That peoples toil for fire,And nations grow weary for nothing?

14 "For the earth will be filled
    With the knowledge of the glory of the Lord,
    As the waters cover the sea.

15 "Woe to you who make your neighbors drink,
    Who mix in your venom even to make them drunk
    So as to look on their nakedness!

16 "You will be filled with disgrace rather than honor.
    Now you yourself drink and expose your own nakedness.
    The cup in the Lord's right hand will come around to you,
    And utter disgrace will come upon your glory.

17 "For the violence [o]done to Lebanon will overwhelm you,
    And the devastation of its beasts by which you terrified them,
    Because of human bloodshed and violence done to the land,
    To the town and all its inhabitants.

18 "What profit is the idol when its maker has carved it,

Or an image, a teacher of falsehood?
For its maker trusts in his own handiwork
When he fashions speechless idols.

19 "Woe to him who says to a piece of wood, 'Awake!'
To a mute stone, 'Arise!'And that is your teacher?
Behold, it is overlaid with gold and silver,
And there is no breath at all inside it.

20 "But the Lord is in His holy temple.
Let all the earth be silent before Him."

Habakkuk 3
New American Standard Bible (NASB)

God's Deliverance of His People

1 A prayer of Habakkuk the prophet, according to Shigionoth.

2 Lord, I have heard the report about You and I fear.
O Lord, revive Your work in the midst of the years,
In the midst of the years make it known;
In wrath remember mercy.

3 God comes from Teman,
And the Holy One from Mount Paran. Selah.
His splendor covers the heavens,
And the earth is full of His praise.

4 His radiance is like the sunlight;
He has rays flashing from His hand,
And there is the hiding of His power.

5 Before Him goes pestilence,
And plague comes after Him.

6   He stood and surveyed the earth;
     He looked and startled the nations.
     Yes, the perpetual mountains were shattered,
     The ancient hills collapsed.
     His ways are everlasting.

7   I saw the tents of Cushan under distress,
     The tent curtains of the land of Midian were trembling.

8   Did the Lord rage against the rivers,
     Or was Your anger against the rivers,
     Or was Your wrath against the sea,
     That You rode on Your horses,
     On Your chariots of salvation?

9   Your bow was made bare,
     The rods of chastisement were sworn. Selah.
     You cleaved the earth with rivers.

10   The mountains saw You and quaked;
     The downpour of waters swept by.
     The deep uttered forth its voice,
     It lifted high its hands.

11   Sun and moon stood in their places;
     They went away at the light of Your arrows,
     At the radiance of Your gleaming spear.

12   In indignation You marched through the earth;
     In anger You trampled the nations.

13   You went forth for the salvation of Your people,
     For the salvation of Your anointed.
     You struck the head of the house of the evil
     To lay him open from thigh to neck. Selah.

14   You pierced with his own spears
     The head of his throngs.
     They stormed in to scatter us;
     Their exultation was like those
     Who devour the oppressed in secret.

15   You trampled on the sea with Your horses,
     On the surge of many waters.

16   I heard and my inward parts trembled,
At the sound my lips quivered.
Decay enters my bones,
And in my place I tremble.
Because I must wait quietly for the day of distress,
For the people to arise who will invade us.

17   Though the fig tree should not blossom
And there be no fruit on the vines,
Though the yield of the olive should fail
And the fields produce no food,
Though the flock should be cut off from the fold
And there be no cattle in the stalls,

18   Yet I will exult in the Lord,
I will rejoice in the God of my salvation.

19   The Lord God is my strength,
And He has made my feet like hinds' feet,
And makes me walk on my high places.

For the choir director, on my stringed instruments.

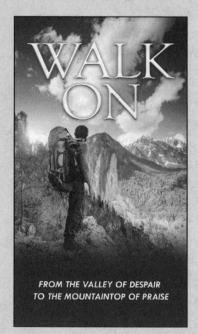

FROM THE VALLEY OF DESPAIR
TO THE MOUNTAINTOP OF PRAISE